You'll read it over and over again. It'll be a tool to keep your marriage fresh, your love alive, your compassion renewed. You'll have a renewed commitment to walk in your marriage like Christ does toward the Church.

So as we plead Jesus' Blood over them it becomes a tangible place, a safe place for them in the spiritual realm.

Those who may have plans to abuse children may exhibit some characteristics:
• They may be loaners. To women this man might seem shy, which can make him appealing.

You'll enjoy the award winning inspirational topical poetry interspersed throughout ANOINTED Married Christian Men.

ANOINTED Married Christian Men

BOOKS and SERVICES
Looking Through The Eyes of Love (Poetry)
Overcomers In Life (A Study Guide)
Abominations to God
A Toilet in the House of God

The Purposeful Parenting Program featuring (c) 2009 the C.E.L.I.A. (Consistently Emotional Life Interconnected Analogy) a combination of philosophical approaches to parenting which can be taught in a variety of programs. If you are interested in attending classes or want to host a seminar at your facility contact Celia. Look for the Purposeful Parenting Program DVD and related materials.

Some of the poems featured in this book are available in laminated pocket cards. Chapters of this book can be purchased separately. Celia is available for Transformational Servant Leadership Training, Emotional Awareness, Urban Youth Trauma, and Pre-Marital Classes, and Spiritual Guidance. Contact, Chaplain Wilson, your internationally certified prevention specialist. (By appointment only.)

Contact Information:
ilisten7ccw@yahoo.com
celia@purposefulparent.biz
P.O. Box 20264
Cleveland, OH 44120-8127
www.purposefulparent.biz

Celia Wilson

ANOINTED MARRIED CHRISTIAN MEN is a novel idea. It shares what marriage is from the viewpoint of the relationship between King Saul and David, while empowering couples. It provides information and examples of Spiritual Warfare (a spiritual hedge and pleading the blood of Jesus over your mate and your marriage). It discusses abuse, sex, and protecting our children from pedophiles. While this book is geared toward wives it will actually be an aid to anyone in a relationship or who plans to be some day.

According to Gene the fact that husbands need to realize how their wives view them was an important motivation for him to read this book. He believes husbands can be available to help their wives with chores and be glad to so, because this creates unity. He explained that being a husband is a twenty-four hour job and it makes wives feel good, appreciated, loved, and interesting when her husband takes and makes the time to work alongside her. He went on to say that often the work becomes times of fun and enjoyment, mainly because they are spending quality time together. Gene loves to help his wife with chores because the faster those things are completed the more time they have to spend ALONE. (Environmental Manager)

ANOINTED Married Christian Men

Annette, who is a friend of the author and the inspiration for the chapter "When to Seek Professional Assistance", read this book when she was going through a tumultuous time in her marriage. She was torn between staying and leaving as she suffered physical and psychological (mental and emotional) abuse at the hands of her Christian husband, who was an Elder in their church.

Annette was wise to continuously seek Spiritual Guidance. Unfortunately, she was encouraged to stay married and told she would not be allowed to be remarried in her home church if she left her husband, which was spiritual abuse. She sought other spiritual support along with scripture and prayer.

She loved her husband. Reading this book helped her understand him within a spiritual framework. She also started to see her "self" from a holistic standpoint as she gained the skills and support she needed. Her wisdom, strength, and self-preservation instincts lead her to put some distance between herself and the danger. She reasoned that the only way to survive was to divorce her husband. She made it out alive, Praise God!
(Executive Office Administrator)

Celia Wilson

ACKNOWLEDGEMENTS

To my husband, Ivan, whose name means "Grace". Thank you for loving me and for being a long suffering patient man. Your gentleness towards me is amazing. Thank you for being an example of grace and for covering me with grace, Honey. Forgive me for the times I didn't see it or honor it. You are my lord and I love you more than I can ever say.

To Amina Diop, thank you for helping me get started. You know I couldn't have done this without you. I appreciate your expertise. I miss you.

To my Chaplain Sisters: Betty Martin Holden, MA, Lay Ecclesial Minister, my wise mentor, sister, partner, friend, I love and honor you in the Lord for being ever faithful. Denise Jenkins, Apostle, AA, RA, always remember your work and labor in the Lord is not in vain, ever. I love you. Thank you both for knowing and speaking into my life to focus on God's gift within me: to use it to bless others. You are truly gifts from God.

ANOINTED Married Christian Men

DEDICATION

This book is dedicated to my Lord and Savior, Jesus Christ. Thank you, Lord for teaching me how to be a better wife and for never giving up on me.

In loving memory of my grandfather, the patriarch of my family, who was 90 when he died. You were by no means perfect. You paid your dues. You were blessed, protected, and forgiven. Thank you for the gift of my mother, Ella, who gave me life.

Vreeland Williams - January 4, 2006

ANOINTED Married Christian Men
By
Chaplain Celia Wilson, MA, OCPSII, CDCA

Published by Celia Wilson © 2010
Cleveland, OH 44128

ISBN: 978-0615-40429-5

Unauthorized use, reproduction is prohibited in all formats and medias by copyright law unless express written consent is given by the author.

God, Jesus, Holy Spirit and all pronouns referring to them are purposefully capitalized by the author.

Unless otherwise noted Scriptures are taken from:
The Amplified Bible, Zondervan Bible Publishing, Grand Rapids, Michigan © 1965
The Open Bible King James Version, Thomas Nelson Publishers, New York, New York © 1985

Definitions are taken from:
Smith's Bible Dictionary © 1987
Random House Dictionary © 1978

Scriptures in Chapter 6 "WHAT'S SEX GOT TO DO WITH IT?" are taken from:
The Amplified Bible, Zondervan Bible Publishing, Grand Rapids, Michigan © 1965
The Open Bible King James Version, Thomas Nelson Publishers, New York, New York © 1985
The Holy Bible: New King James Version © 1982, Thomas Nelson, Inc.

Definitions in Chapter 6 are taken from:
Merriam-Webster's Collegiate Dictionary, Eleventh Edition © 2003 Springfield, Massachusetts

All poems used with author's permission are from:
Looking Through the Eyes of Love © 1996 Celia Price-Wilson

Disclaimer: No names were used in Chapter 8. If someone believes their story was told please know that these things happen daily all over our country. If something like this occurred in your family you certainly are not alone and Celia empathizes with you, but due to the nature of Chaplain Wilson's work she has come in contact with hundreds of cases of abuse.

Font: Calibri

Price: US Currency $16.00

© 2010 by Celia Wilson: Cleveland, OH 44128

The Blurb-provided layout designs and graphic elements are copyright Blurb Inc., 2010. This book was created using the Blurb creative publishing service. The book author retains sole copyright to his or her contributions to this book.

blurb

blurb.com

TABLE OF CONTENTS

CHAPTER 1 — 12
The Perfect Christian Husband
Scriptures to Pray for Your Husband — 20
Scriptures for You — 26

CHAPTER 2 — 29
God Anointed Husbands
Introduction — 31

CHAPTER 3 — 59
What is a Hedge and How To Pray One For Someone?
Prayer for You (I) — 64

CHAPTER 4 — 68
How to Plead the Blood of Jesus
Prayer for You (II) — 97
Pleading the Blood of Jesus Over Your Husband — 100

CHAPTER 5 — 103
When To Seek Professional Assistance
This is Abuse — 114
Prayer for You (III) — 119

CHAPTER 6 — 123
The Significance and Power of "Without Spot or Blemish"

CHAPTER 7 150
What's Sex Got to Do with It? 213
Prayer for You (IV)
CHAPTER 8 217
Anointed Men and Our Kids

CHAPTER 1
THE PREFECT CHRISTIAN HUSBAND

Celia Wilson

Statistics on Christian Divorce and Domestic Violence

In a 2009 report by Ontario Consultants on Religious Tolerance on the website religioustolerance.org the following data exists:

Barna report: Variation in divorce rates among Christian faith groups:

Denomination (order of decreasing divorce rate) % who have been divorced:

Non-denominational **34%   Baptists 29%
Mainline Protestants   25%   Mormons 24%
Catholics   21%   Lutherans 21%

** Barna uses the term "non-denominational" to refer to Evangelical Christian congregations that are not affiliated with a specific denomination.
The vast majority are fundamentalist in their theological beliefs.

Variation in divorce rates by Religion % have been divorced:

Jews   30%   Born-again Christians 27%
Other Christians 24%   Atheists, Agnostics 21%

ANOINTED Married Christian Men

Data reported on domesticviolencestatistics.org:

• Every 9 seconds a U.S. woman is assaulted or beaten.
• Around the world, at least one in three women has been beaten, coerced into sex or otherwise abused during her lifetime. Most often, the abuser is a member of her own family.
• Everyday in the U.S., more than three women are murdered by their husbands or boyfriends.
• Nearly 1 in 5 teenage girls who have been in a relationship said a boyfriend threatened violence or self-harm if presented with a breakup.
• Studies suggest that up to 10 million children witness some form of domestic violence annually.
• Domestic violence victims lose nearly 8 million days of paid work per year in the U.S. alone—the equivalent of 32,000 full-time jobs.
• Based on reports from 10 countries, between 55 percent and 95 percent of women who had been physically abused by their partners had never contacted non-governmental organizations, shelters, or the police for help.
• The costs of intimate partner violence in the U.S. alone exceed $5.8 billion per year: $4.1 billion are for direct medical and health care services, while productivity losses account for nearly $1.8 billion.
• Men who as children witnessed their parents'

Celia Wilson

domestic violence were twice as likely to abuse their own wives, than sons of nonviolent parents.
• Ninety-two percent of women surveyed listed reducing domestic violence and sexual assault as their top concern.

To My Husband

I have prayed so long for you,
At times I didn't know what to do,
But now you're here, by my side,
Together we'll love, care, and abide.
To make you happy and see you smile.
To sit and hug, or cuddle a while.
To please your spirit, body, and soul.
To minister to you, my love, as a whole.
To meet each need that you might have,
And every day to make you laugh.
If in our lives these things I fulfill,
I would have truly done God's will.

National Library of Poetry Award Winner

ANOINTED Married Christian Men

One night as I was working at the kitchen sink the Holy Spirit began to talk with me.

He said that Proverbs 18:22 says, "He who finds a wife, finds a good thing and obtains favor of the Lord."

He told me I was a good thing to my husband, because I was fulfilling my wifely duty by the work I was performing in the kitchen.

I agreed. I told Him that we used Proverbs 18:22 on our wedding invitations, so my husband *must* think I'm a good thing. After all it was his idea to use that scripture. I thought with some attitude that my husband's favor with the Lord must be his ability to sit in the living room chilling out doing nothing, while I worked alone in the kitchen.

I asked Him, "Why, if my husband thought I was a good thing was he allowing me to work in the kitchen by myself, while he sat in the living room doing nothing?"

He again told me I was a good thing and a gift to my husband.

I said, "Right." I found myself starting to get angry. I said, "Since I'm a good thing, then my husband should be a good thing. If he was a good thing he would get up and come in here to keep me company." I was thinking about James 1:17 which says, "Every good and perfect gift is from above, and comes down from the Father of lights."

The Holy Spirit said, "You know your husband

Celia Wilson

is a good man. Think about all the good things he does."

So I did. I went down the list of things he does that are good in my mind. I also went down the list of things he doesn't do that are good.

The Holy Spirit said, "No matter how mad you get at him, he is still a gift from God to you. God made him just for you."

I said, "Right." My anger came to a slight roar inside. I thought about James 1:17 again and my spirit was in shock. I told the Holy Spirit, "My husband was good, but he wasn't perfect." Now I was questioning whether my husband and I should really be together. Mind you, I never once considered the fact that I wasn't perfect. Nor did I consider the fact that the definition of the word "perfect" in scripture doesn't mean "perfect- without flaw", but mature. Even if I had my husband was not really mature: but in so many areas he was more mature than me. Anyway, I wondered how my husband could be a gift from the Father according to scripture and be good, but imperfect.

That's when the Holy Spirit said, "Your husband was created a spiritual being first."

> Genesis 1:27-28, God created man in his own image, in the image of God created he him: male and female created he them. And God blessed them, and God said unto them, be

fruitful and multiply, and replenish the earth, and subdue it: and have dominion over the fish of the sea, and over the fowl of the air, and over every living thing that moveth upon the earth.

At this point your husband was perfect just as this spiritual man and woman were perfect. As yet they had no fleshly bodies. Genesis 2:7, "And the Lord God formed man of the dust of the ground, and breathed into his nostrils the breath of life; and man became a living soul." Now, the formed man with a living soul is vulnerable. He is still perfect though, because sin has not yet entered the world.

He said, "Celia, your husband's spirit was perfect when I first created it, but during his life his spirit has been subjected to many derogatory words: from his childhood, throughout his school days, his years in the military, in his work situations, and in his marriage to you. As soon as his spirit was put into his fleshly body he became a living soul. Things have been said and done each day to adversely affect his perfection or completeness. Each day of his life someone strips away some of the perfect spirit I gave him. If you want to see the perfect-ness, the completeness in your husband, you have to start confessing what My Word says about him in order to heal and combat all the negative and derogatory words that have entered into his spirit."

Celia Wilson

He told me I had to realize my job was to guide my house according to I Timothy 5:14, "I will therefore that the younger women marry, bear children, guide (rule) the house, give none occasion to the adversary to speak reproachfully."

I replied, "I am guiding my house."

He said, "Not when you're screaming and yelling."

He asked, "How would you lead a blind person somewhere?"

I described how I would take the person gently by the arm and slowly lead him/her along the way.

The Holy Spirit said, "That's right, you would not run up to the blind person grab him by the arm and start yanking him down the street, because he would resist you and rebel against your leading. Why? Because he'd feel threatened and unsafe wouldn't he?"

I said, "Yes."

He explained, "That is exactly what you do when you yell at your husband. When you yell in your house you are not guiding it. If you want him to do something you must gently lead him into doing it. You have to make gentle suggestions. When you start guiding your house properly you will see the good perfect husband God gave you."

ANOINTED Married Christian Men

SCRIPTURES TO PRAY FOR YOUR HUSBAND

Celia Wilson

These are scriptures He gave me to meditate on, memorize, and say concerning what I speak about my husband.

> I Timothy 3:2-11, A bishop (man) then must be blameless, the husband of one wife, vigilant, sober, of good behavior, given to hospitality, apt to teach: Not given to wine, no striker, not greedy of filthy lucre, but patient, not a brawler, not covetous; One that ruleth well his own house, having his children in subjection with all gravity; For if a man know not how to rule his own house, how shall he take care of the church of God? Moreover he must have a good report of them which are without; lest he fall into reproach and the snare of the devil. Likewise must the deacons (men) be grave, not double-tongued, not given to much wine, not greedy of filthy lucre; Holding the mystery of the faith in pure conscience. Even so must their wives be grave, not slanders, sober, faithful in all things. Let the deacons (men) be the husbands of one wife, ruling their children and their own houses well.
> Words in parentheses are my insertion.

Some husbands have ex-wives and baby mama

ANOINTED Married Christian Men

drama.
Some husbands beat their wives and fight regularly.
Some husbands have alcohol and other addiction problems.

I Timothy 2:8, "I will therefore that men pray everywhere, lifting up holy hands, without wrath and doubting.

Some husbands don't pray.
Some husbands do pray, but are so wrathful and have no faith in what they pray.
Some husbands doubt themselves.

Ephesians 5:23-29, For the husband is the head of the wife, even as Christ is the head of the church: and he is the savior of the body. Husbands love your wives, even as Christ also loved the church, and gave himself for it. That he might sanctify and cleanse it with the washing of water by the word. That he might present it to himself a glorious church (wife), not having spot, or wrinkle, or any such thing; but that it (she) should be holy and without blemish. So ought men to love their own bodies, he that loveth his wife, loveth himself. For no man ever yet hated his own flesh; but nourisheth and cherisheth it, even as the Lord the church.
Words in parentheses are my insertion.

Some men hate their bodies, their own flesh so how

can they love their wives properly.
Some men don't speak the Word or any positive words over, to, or into their wives: they don't praise.
Some husbands are working their wives to death, stressing them to death.
Some husbands are not ensuring their wives are living without spot, blemish, or wrinkle.

I Corinthians 7:2, Let every man have his own wife. Let the husband render unto the wife due benevolence: The wife hath not power of her own body, but the husband: and likewise also the husband hath not power of his own body, but the wife. Defraud ye not one the other, except it be with consent for a time, that ye may give yourselves to fasting and prayer; and come together again, that Satan tempt you not for your incontinency. (This means no withholding of sex from our spouses because we are angry or whatever). But he that is married careth for the things that are of the world, how he may please his wife.
Words in parentheses are my insertion.

Proverbs 12:14, "A man shall be satisfied with good by the fruit of his mouth: and the recompense of a man's hands shall be rendered unto him."

Some husbands are unemployed or underemployed, or have given up and don't want to work.
Many men have street skills, but don't know how to

ANOINTED Married Christian Men

translate that into lucrative marketable skills.
Then there are men who constantly speak evil and
negativity into their lives and into their wives.
Still, there are men who care for their own things but
not how to please their wives.
Some men earn more than enough, but are stingy
with their wives or lie about their income.

Proverbs 31:11, 28, "The heart of her husband doth safely trust in her, so that he shall have no need of spoil. Her children arise up, and call her blessed; her husband also, and he praiseth her."

Some husbands don't trust in or have confidence in their wives or their abilities, in fact; they are extremely jealous and possessive. They verbally degrade them, regularly. Again, notice that praising is important.

Proverbs 5:18-19, "Let thy fountains be blessed; and rejoice with the wife of thy youth. Let her be as the loving hind (a timid, maternal, modest, gentle animal), and the pleasant roe (lovely gazelle): and be thou ravished always with her love." (Amplified)

Some husbands are not rejoicing they are complaining, blaming, cussing, and fussing.

Genesis 2:24, "Therefore shall a man leave his father

and mother, and shall cleave unto his wife; and they shall be one flesh."

Some husbands have "Friends", girlfriends and best friends who are female. They put some other females before their wives including their mothers, sisters, and daughters. Putting male friends before a wife is also not in the best interest of the marriage.

Ecclesiastes 9:9, "Live joyfully with the wife whom thou loveth all the days of the life of thy vanity, which he hath given thee under the sun, all the days of thy vanity; for that is thy portion in this life, and in thy labor which thou takest under the sun."

Some husbands make their homes a living hell. They torture their wives mentally and some physically. They yell making their wives and children live in fear. After the wedding day, the joy is gone.

Isaiah 54:5, "For your husband is your Maker."

Some husbands do not understand that they have the power to make their wives. The power to make his wife lies in his mouth (what he says about her and to her). The power to make her lies in the way he spends money on her and the quality of the time he spends with her.

ANOINTED Married Christian Men

SCRIPTURES FOR YOU

Celia Wilson

    These are the scriptures the Lord gave me to help me become better at saying and doing what I have to regarding my husband, regardless of what I think about him, his behavior, or lack thereof. If I believe the Word of God, and I do, then I have the faith to speak, believing God's Word will work in my husband's life. God will work His Word therein as I do so. I hope they bless you in your quest to live and love God's Anointed men.

Matthew 12:26, "But I say unto you, that every idle word that men shall speak, they shall give account thereof in the Day of Judgment."

Ephesians 5:26, "Be ye angry, and sin not; let not the sun go down upon your wrath."

Proverbs 18:21, "Death and life are in the power of the tongue, and they that love it shall eat the fruit thereof."

James 3:10, "Out of the same mouth proceedeth blessing and cursing. My brethren, these things ought not so to be."

Jeremiah 6:2, "I have likened thee daughter of Zion (You) to a comely and delicate woman."
Word in parentheses is my insertion.

Deuteronomy 18:13, "Thou shalt be perfect with the

Lord thy God."

Psalm 39:1, "I said I will take heed to my ways; that I sin not with my tongue."

Psalm 37:8, "Cease from anger, and forsake wrath, fret not thyself in any wise to do evil."

CHAPTER 2
GOD ANOINTED
HUSBANDS

ANOINTED Married Christian Men

Loving You

I'm a woman born and bred.
Feeling good from my feet to my head.
This feeling's not coming from some man's bed,
Because I love myself.

As a woman I'm versatile as can be.
I do not mind letting my man lead me.
In conversation, laughter, and lifestyle I'm free,
Because I love me.

My looks, appetites, and dreams are mine.
And I will do what I can in my life time,
To be there, to encourage you, and see you through,
Because by loving me, I'm able to love you.

Celia Wilson

INTRODUCTION

ANOINTED Married Christian Men

    This section of this book is directed to all married Christian men and women, that is why the Holy Spirit has led me to be straight forward about some major points. These points will be addressed first so when we get into the study we have some foundation to build upon.

James 5:16, "Confess your faults one to another, and pray one for another that ye may be healed. The effectual fervent prayer of a righteous man availeth much."

    The first thing we must realize, as wives, is no husband is without flaw. The key is for the wife to pray for her husband's flaws without criticizing or belittling him. When we pray we must realize he will be healed. Our prayers bring about much change.

Philippians 4:13, "I have strength for all things in Christ who empowers me – I am ready for anything and equal to anything through Him Who infuses inner strength into me, (that is, I am self-sufficient in Christ's sufficiency)." (Amplified)

    Secondly, a wife must realize Jesus empowers her with enough inner strength to handle anything her husband might do, while God is in the process of maturing him. Instead of concentrating on the negative remember this scripture.

Celia Wilson

Philippians 4:6-8, Do not fret or have any anxiety about anything, but in every circumstance and in everything by prayer and petition (definite requests) with thanksgiving continue to make your wants known to God. And God's peace (be yours, that tranquil state of a soul assured of its salvation through Christ, and so fearing nothing from God and content with its earthly lot of whatever sort that is, that peace) which transcends all understanding, shall garrison and mount guard over your hearts and minds in Christ Jesus. For the rest, brethren, whatever is true, whatever is worthy of reverence and is honorable and seemly, whatever is just, whatever is pure, whatever is lovely and lovable, whatever is winsome and gracious, if there is any virtue and excellence, if there is anything worthy of praise, think on and weigh and take account of these things – fix your minds on them. (Amplified)

Also, we must let Jesus love our husbands through us.

I Corinthians 14:4-8, Love endures long and is patient and kind; love never is envious nor boils over with jealousy: is not boastful or vainglorious, does not display itself haughtily. It is not conceited – arrogant and inflated with pride: it is not rude (unmannerly), and does not act unbecomingly. Love (God's love in us) does not insist on its own rights or its own way, for it is not self-seeking; it takes no account of the wrong done to it – pays no attention to a suffered wrong. It does not rejoice at injustices and unrighteousness, but rejoices when right and truth prevail. Love bears up under anything and everything that comes; is ever ready to believe the best of every person, its hopes are fadeless under all circumstances and it endures everything (without weakening). Love never fails – never fades out or becomes obsolete or comes to an end. (Amplified)

Praise God for His Word to women about their husbands. Praise God for His Word to men about themselves. God anointed husbands to hold the position as Head of Household and as the Head of his wife.

I Corinthians 11:3 KJV, "But I would have you know that the head of every man is Christ; and the head of the woman is the man; and the head of Christ is

God."

Ephesians 5:23 KJV, "For the husband is the head of the wife, even as Christ is the head of the church…"

I pray this foundation of scriptures regarding the marriage relationship will give you even greater understanding as we get into our study of the anointing on married Christian men.

ANOINTED Married Christian Men

ANOINTED Married Christian Men was revealed to me out of the text or within the text of I Samuel 18, in the relationship between King Saul and David. I know I never would have seen or understood a marriage relationship by looking into the relationship of these two men, but God in His infinite wisdom chose to reveal this to me by His Spirit.

In I Samuel 18 King Saul invites David to live in his home because of the great presence of God that surrounded David. Since David had killed the giant Philistine, King Saul had a need to be near David. We are going to look at the relationship. King Saul will be the example of the husband and David will be the example of the wife. At the conclusion we will appreciate and respect the role, the position that God has given to husbands.

I Samuel 18:5, "...and David was very obedient to Saul and behaved himself wisely."

This is how marriages usually start out. The wife goes out of her way to please her new husband and her new husband can't stand to be without his new darling mate. They think about each other constantly. No problem, right?

I Corinthians 7:33-34, "But he that is married careth for the things that are of the world, how he may please his wife. There is difference also between a wife and a virgin. The unmarried woman careth for the things of the Lord, that she may be holy both in body and in spirit; but she that is married careth for the things of the world, how she may please her husband."

I Samuel 18:6-9 (Paraphrased by me) - One day David came back from battle and the women of the town were praising him and singing songs about his greatness because he was victorious. However, they mentioned the fact that David killed more men than King Saul. So from that day King Saul was suspicious and jealous of David.

      This is the next step in some marriages, also. We are praised by others for being a good wife, or something good happens in our life, or we get pregnant and all the attention is focused on us. Maybe we've been home all day cooking, cleaning, taking care of the home, and/or kids, or maybe after we've been working at our job all day we come home to handle all the household stuff, including the kids. Either way our husbands have two choices when they come into the home. They can rejoice and get involved with us or they can get an attitude allowing uncomfortable feelings to influence them. King Saul didn't rejoice with David: he chose the latter route.

I Peter 3:7 says, "Likewise, ye husbands, dwell with

them (the wives) according to knowledge, giving honor unto the wife, as unto the weaker vessel, and as being heirs together of the grace of life; that your prayers be not hindered." Words in parentheses are my insertion.

If a husband has never washed a dish, cooked a meal, washed clothes, picked up stuff and cleaned up the house, sewn clothes, taken care of children (feeding, changing, doing homework, fixing scrapes, sitting up at night) doing all the things his wife does, he is not dwelling with her according to knowledge, because he does not know what it feels like to handle or juggle all these things. If he has not studied to acquire knowledge regarding how her body works, for instance, when she becomes pregnant or pre-menopausal he is not dwelling with her according to knowledge because he doesn't understand her. If he were dwelling with her according to knowledge he would honor her. The knowledge would almost necessitate he honor her, because her role is very important, very difficult, and can be extremely tiring.

The Bible says we're "the weaker vessel" because we lose blood monthly which drains our iron, affects our hormones, causes some of us pain, causes bloating, and other complex symptoms. Usually our frames aren't as strong as men's, but this fact in no way suggests that some women are not physically strong and capable of doing whatever a man can do. However, the biological and physical feats our bodies endure are worthy of honor from our husbands. Because we are both (individually and as a couple) heirs of the grace of life as Christians, if he does not live with his wife according to knowledge his prayers will be hindered. Wow. If his prayers are hindered the household will suffer. If his prayers are hindered his wife has to pray even more, because there will be negative consequences for the family.

I Samuel 18:10, "Next day an evil spirit from God came mightily upon Saul, and he raved (madly) in his house." (Amplified)

So, we see that God allowed an evil spirit to come on King Saul. Would you say his prayers were hindered at this point? We see how an evil spirit was affecting King Saul in a rather ungodly manner. Let's see how an evil spirit could affect a Christian husband. The next day the husband we introduced earlier wakes up with an attitude, loses his temper, or has a bad disposition with his wife because he allowed those feelings of jealously, anger, or mistrust to stew within his spirit all night. Remember, earlier when I was in the kitchen working by myself – I was feeling jealous and angry. As humans we are not immune from these feelings, but it's what we do after we recognize we are operating in these spirits that matters.

In this particular instance the husband and King Saul allowed the Devil to have place in their lives (Ephesians 4:27). Ephesians 4:26, "Be ye angry, and sin not: let not the sun go down upon your wrath." We are human. We will get angry, but it's what we do when we are angry that counts. We have to use everything within us to avoid sinning in anger. Many husbands use their size, positions, or the prejudice of archaic patriarchal beliefs as reasons to act badly, mistreat their wives, talk down to them, and treat them as if they are children. Their behavior is far from honoring to their wives.

I Samuel 18:12, "And Saul was scared of David, because the Lord was with him, and was gone from Saul."

The husband is upset, scared, or jealous because God is blessing the wife more abundantly, more quickly, maybe, than him. Maybe he's afraid his wife is disrespecting him; will see him as weak in some way because he is tired; or he made a bad decision, or he messed up in some way. It is possible that he'd experience these feelings if he doesn't realize his wife's blessings - bless him. I Corinthians 12:25-26, "That there should be no schism (division) in the body; but that the members should have the same care one for another. And whether one member suffer; all the members suffer with it; or one

Celia Wilson

member be honored, all the members rejoice with it." Word in parentheses is my insertion. Imagine if King Saul had realized David's ability to fight and win was a blessing to him and his kingdom. If he had rejoiced in this knowledge and David's ability we could end this book right here, but we can't because he didn't and maybe our husbands aren't either.

In a marriage it is alright - normal - even healthy for each person to have their own things, such as golf clubs, videos, or whatever. However, if we're looking at our lives from a Kingdom Perspective (God's Family Kingdom), I mean with the understanding that all we have comes from God and as a couple everything we own is OURS, not his and hers or mine and yours this changes the way we describe our belongings. With the kingdom perspective those who are married perceive everything in their relationship as the common possession of the couple. This eliminates the need to argue about, "You are not driving my car, you are not eating my cake, I'm not watching your kids, etc." In Acts 4:32 we read, "And the multitude of them that believed were of one heart (spirit) and of one soul (mind): neither said any of them that aught of the things which he possessed was his own; but they had all things in common." Words in parentheses are my insertion. As a Christian husband or wife, as a believer are we of one mind and spirit with our spouse regarding one another's talents, gifts, belongings, desires, needs, etc.? If not, can we see how (like King

ANOINTED Married Christian Men

Saul) we can be influenced by an evil spirit? It is definitely an evil spirit that would tell a husband his wife's blessing is a threat to him or his manhood.

Note: This is not the course I would take if I were a man or woman of excessive means, really rich marrying someone who is not. This might anger some readers, but there are wolves in sheep's clothing who sometimes attach themselves to you just to get your money. Pre-nups stop all that. I know many people think this is a modern marriage issue which demonstrates a lack of trust, but those born into royalty who marry sign papers and marriage agreements all the time. Many African, Asian, East Indian, as well as, European cultures have customs regarding marriage agreements which have existed for centuries. They're still widely used today. That money and property would be my children's legacy. It is my Godly responsibility to guard, manage, and protect my children's future.

    I digress. Let's get back to the story. From this point on King Saul is trying to kill David every chance he gets. Husband's operating under this kind of spiritual oppression try to kill their wife's spirit, zeal, joy, and confidence every chance they get.

I Samuel 23:16, "Jonathan, Saul's son (Who was very close – like a blood brother to David) got up, went to

Celia Wilson

David and encouraged (strengthen) his hand in the Lord." Words in parentheses are my insertion.

Wives, we can thank God for our sisters in Christ who encourage us to not give up on our marriages or our husbands. I Thessalonians 5:11, "Wherefore comfort yourselves, and edify one another, even as also ye do." This is critical. If the women we are talking to are downing or berating our husband's because of their negative traits they are not edifying us, our spouses or, our marriages. Cease these conversations because we don't need any help focusing on the negative. We can do that all by ourselves. The challenge here is to ensure the people in our lives help us focus on the WORD of GOD as it pertains to us individually, our husbands, and our marriages.

I Samuel 23:29, "David dwelt in strongholds."

In the Random House Dictionary a "stronghold" is a well fortified place. In this verse of scripture the word means "fortress". Christian wives need to have a well fortified place or fortress in which to hide away when their husbands are raving mad. When they are not exhibiting Christian characteristics like the Fruit of the Spirit found in Galatians 5:22, 23. The well fortified fortress is in prayer and in the knowledge of the Word. Prayer

ANOINTED Married Christian Men

and praying the Word of God will be essential to a wife in this situation. Jeremiah 1:12 says, "For I will hasten my word to perform it." Since God watches over His Word to make sure it happens we need to speak it out when our men want to argue. This arguing should not be verbally or sexually abusive. When we think we can't contain or maintain our peace a second longer just say what the Word says. It will work. There are scriptures at the end of this study to learn, pray, and say everyday concerning Christian husbands.

     Some may be asking why this book is entitled "ANOINTED Married Christian Men" since there really hasn't been that much said about these husbands being anointed. Have patience. The Lord will make everything plain as we proceed. In Matthew 19:6 the scripture reads, "What therefore God hath joined together, let not man put asunder." This is relevant for those couples who say we were not saved when we got married, so God did not join us together. If we got saved after we were already married then our marriage is new in Christ Jesus, also. All Christian couples have to realize God is in the marriage fixing business. He fixes wives and husbands; divorce court doesn't. As God's women we need to stop running away from the devil when he attacks our marriages and stand up to fight for the men we love.

*I Samuel 24:*6, "*And he said unto his men. The Lord*

Celia Wilson

forbid that I should do this thing unto my master, the LORD'S ANOINTED, to stretch forth mine hand against him, seeing he is the ANOINTED OF THE LORD."

This is David speaking about King Saul. David had a chance to either hurt or get rid of Saul, but he wouldn't because King Saul was the LORD'S ANOINTED. We may ask, how can this be when I Samuel 18:10, 12 told us about Saul being taken over by an evil spirit and how God had departed from him? How could he still be considered the LORD'S ANOINTED? The reason David said this, and was correct in saying it, is because God still ANOINTED SAUL TO BE KING. King Saul was still the Head of Israel (anointed to lead, make decisions for the betterment, and survival of Israel).

Christian husbands may not always act like what our fantasy of a man of God should be, but the wives of these men must remember GOD ANOINTED THEM TO BE THE HEADS OF THEIR HOUSEHOLDS AND HEADS OF THEIR WIVES. How many of us know it takes much wisdom, discernment, negotiations, diplomacy, and strength to guide a nation? Well, it takes all these things to lead a family, too. Ask a single mother what it takes. Women were not meant to head households, men were. That is God's perfect order for the family. That is not to say He won't bless diverse familial situations. Wives must

ANOINTED Married Christian Men

respect the husband's God given position. David may not have had a reason to respect the man King Saul had become, but he had enough wisdom to realize that he still had to respect the King's position. When we find ourselves about to disrespect our husband's position this is when entering our stronghold is appropriate. Praying and saying what the Word says, believing God can fix him and the situation. Isaiah 55:11 reads, "So shall my word be that goeth forth out of my mouth, it shall not return unto me void, but it shall accomplish that which I please, and it shall prosper in the thing whereto I sent it." Our husbands were made, created to stand in the position as our leaders.

First Lady Michelle Obama said of her husband, President Barack Obama, he has a host of very intelligent and knowledgeable people to advise him. I'm not quoting her verbatim. The essence of what she said that we and our ANOINTED HUSBANDS need to remember is: leading doesn't mean ignoring the wife or not consulting her regarding decisions which need to be made. After all I Timothy 5:14 instructs women to guide their homes. That word "guide" is translated "rule". So we rule our homes together. How about this; a wise successful husband values and seeks the advice of his wife just as a wise leader seeks advice. We have the power, authority, and responsibility to send God's Word into our husbands, our marriages, particular situations, or circumstances in our marriages.

I Samuel 26:9, "For who can stretch forth his hand against THE LORD'S ANOINTED, and be guiltless?"

A Christian wife is expected to be a helpmeet to her husband. Will we be found guiltless of the things we, as wives, have done to the men God gave us? Are we yelling at them, calling them ungodly negative names, or talking about them badly behind their back? Are we praying for them? This is our responsibility. Proverbs 31:12, "She will do him good and not evil all the days of her life." Are we doing our husbands good and not evil in word or deed? Think about it.

Wives are helpmeets. We need to know what this means so we can begin to work and live in our capacity. Genesis 2:18 in the Amplified Bible reads, "Now the Lord said, It is not good (sufficient, satisfactory) that the man should be alone; I will make him a HELPER MEET (SUITABLE, ADAPTED, COMPLETING) to him." Are we helping or hurting our husbands? Ask yourself, "Am I suitable or unsuitable, do I fit my particular man?" Are we complementing our husbands or are we chipping away at them? Are we adapting to our husbands or are we trying to change them to fit our idea of what the perfect husband – man should be?

God would not have put us together if we

could not adapt to the man, Your Man. He doesn't eat his eggs the way we like to cook them. We change the way we cook them. He desires sex when we don't. Then we should desire him when he wants sex. Then God can make him desire us when we want sex. Genesis 3:16, "...and thy desire shall be to thy husband, and he shall have rule over thee." God created us to be wives to our particular men, in so doing He made us desire our particular men (our husbands). If he wants sex and we don't he's suppose to be given sex by us regardless of how we feel. I'm not talking about if we are sick. It is God's perfect plan that we desire our husbands. Really, since God said this He will make our husbands answer our desire for intimacy, closeness, affection, love, and sex.

  Also, if we were not suitable for our men, God would not have joined us together. This needs repeating for those of us who like to make excuses. It doesn't matter if we were forced to get married shotgun style. It doesn't matter if we were prostitutes and he was our pimp. The Bible says in II Corinthians 5:17, "Therefore if any man be in Christ he is a new creature (a brand new creation), old things are passed away, behold ALL things (marriages) are become new." Words in parentheses are my insertion. Our men are new, we are new, and our marriages are new. There are no excuses. Looking, expecting, and reacting to him in the old way might also need to stop.

    Divorced and remarried couples can allow the Lord to have this marriage by dedicating it to Him. There is no condemnation. So bringing old guilt and disappointment to a new marriage is unproductive when seeking positive outcomes. Romans 8:1, reads, "There is therefore now no condemnation to them which are in Christ Jesus, who walk not after the flesh, but after the Spirit." However, if we feel convicted maybe that's a signal to make some internal changes without focusing on changing him so much.

I Samuel 26:16, "This thing is not good that thou hast done. As the Lord liveth, ye are worthy to die, because ye have not kept your master, THE LORD'S ANOINTED."

    David said this to Saul's men because they did not protect their King, which enabled David to enter into the middle of Saul's camp where he lay sleeping surrounded by all his sleeping men. As David infiltrated the camp he got up close to Saul right in the middle of the camp where Saul lay sleeping on his pillow. If King Saul's men had been watching and looking out for their King, David wouldn't have gotten that close to him.

    It is the same way in the marriage relationship sometime. If wives would spend more

ANOINTED Married Christian Men

time meditating than mouthing and more time praying than protesting God's men would be protected from many of the enemy's fiery darts. Isaiah 54:17, "No weapon that is formed against thee shall prosper; and every tongue that shall rise against thee in judgment thou shall condemn (prove wrong). This is the heritage of the servants of the Lord, and their righteousness is of me, saith the Lord." Words in parentheses are my insertion. We have the ability and authority to pray a hedge around our husbands and plead Jesus' Blood over every area of our men's lives.

  As Christian wives we have to understand Satan will attack our husbands before attacking anyone else in his household. He knows if he can keep Christian husbands down it will affect the wife and the children, if there are any. It will tear at the family system and order will be destroyed. If what we do in our marriages does not build it by making it Godly, strong, steady, healthy, and positive we are foolish. We are tearing down our own houses. Proverbs 14:1, "Every wise woman buildeth her house: but the foolish plucketh it down (tears down) with her hands." Words in parentheses are my insertion. Someone doesn't want to accept this. Let's repeat it. If we are not building our house, our home, and our husbands up we are tearing them down, period. We can't let the devil use us. Be strong in the Lord and in the power of His might, because if Christian families are weakened the churches effectiveness will also weaken, which will make the entire Body of Christ shaky.

This is Satan's ultimate goal. As wives we are not or shouldn't be ignorant of his devices. We must refuse to be used and manipulated by him at his will. Do we have our husband's back? Can he depend on us and rely on us when the whole world seems to be against him? Revelations 12:17 reads, "And the dragon was wroth with the woman, and went to make war with the remnant of her seed, which keep the commandments of God, and have the testimony of Jesus Christ." Here the dragon is the devil. The woman is the church body. The remnant of her seed is each one of us individually. We can see the devil was angry, enraged at the Body of Christ as a whole. Consequently, he went about to make war with each of us individually, because of our obedience, knowledge, and use of the Gospel of Jesus Christ. We are victorious wives. If we are not walking in victory in our marriages right now, hold on. Help is in our hands. It's within our grasp. Keep reading.

I Samuel 26:33, "The Lord render to every man his righteousness and his faithfulness; for the Lord delivered thee into my hand today, but I (WOULD NOT) stretch forth mine hand against the LORD'S ANOINTED.

The first words to focus on are *would not*.

ANOINTED Married Christian Men

David said I would not, which means he had a choice. It also means it was within his power to say I will or I won't. Wives the same is true concerning us. We can choose to be submissive or chose to be rebels. We can choose to be argumentative or choose to be quiet. It is within our control, our power to leave the house to go for a walk or drive. It is within our power to keep peace within our homes and harmony within our marriages. Notice the use of the "LORD'S ANOINTED" for the 5th time. Five times David calls Kings Saul the Lord's Anointed. In Romans 10:17 we learn that "Faith comes by hearing, and hearing by the Word of God." We need to grab hold of the faith in these words realizing the role of "husband" is an anointed position for men to hold.

The first job God gave Adam concerning other human beings and human relationships was husband.

> Genesis 2:21-25, And the Lord God caused a deep sleep to fall upon Adam, and he slept; and he took one of his ribs, and closed up the flesh thereof; and the rib, which the Lord had taken from man, made he a woman, and brought her unto the man. And Adam said, This is now bone of my bones, and flesh of my flesh: she shall be called Woman, because she was taken out of Man. Therefore shall a man leave his father and his mother, and shall

cleave unto his wife; and they shall be one flesh. And they were naked, the man and his wife, and were not ashamed.

Stunningly, it doesn't say he shall cleave unto his female best friend, his sister, his cousin, or his daughter; he's cleaving unto his WIFE. Therefore, being a husband must be an important job for the man. Once again the question arises, since being a husband is the man's most important position, can't we see why the devil wants to destroy the role man has as husband, head of household, head of wife? If as wives we are faithful and righteous in our duties God will deliver a better husband into our hands. I Thessalonians 5:18 reads, "In EVERYthing give thanks: for this is the will of God in Christ Jesus concerning you." It did not say in every good thing, or in everything we want, or in everything that meets our desires. It just said in everything give thanks. Thank God we are in the present situation. Many times if wives would thank God and be quiet; instead of saying things like, "I told you not to do it that way" or "Why don't you listen to me" or "Go ahead, do it your way, but when you mess everything up don't come back asking me to fix it" God could actually guide and teach her husband the lessons He wants him to learn.

Sometimes wives are lesson blockers. So what if the husband makes a wrong decision. Maybe

ANOINTED Married Christian Men

God wants to teach him how to pray before he makes a decision. Remember, that man is still in process, even though he has to walk in carrying so much responsibility. He hasn't arrived yet. If we get in the way God can't get through. When Mrs. Mouthy Wife breaks in all the husband learns is not to listen to God while blocking us out. Give God a chance to work His perfect work. If - as wives - we respect, uphold, and appreciate the God given anointing upon our husbands God will bless us in our marriage relationships. Hebrews 11:6, "But without faith it is impossible to please him; for he that cometh to God must believe that he is, and that he is a rewarder of them that diligently seek him."

  While we are remembering Hebrews 11:6 remember that "He who finds a wife, finds a good thing, and obtains favor of the Lord", Proverbs 18:22. Internalize this: wives are good things for husbands no matter what he or anyone says. Internalize this: "YOU" are a good thing for your husband regardless of how you feel. Internalize this: wives are good things. It is because of the wife that husbands obtain favor from the Lord. We have to be confident in our position. As wives we need to internalize our goodness and then just "be" good.

I Samuel 30:6, " …but David encouraged himself in the Lord his God."

Celia Wilson

    Once we start respecting our husband's position we'll be able to encourage or strengthen ourselves in the Lord our God as David did, because we'll know WHAT the will of God in Christ Jesus is concerning us? Respecting our husband's position of authority (responsibility) in our lives and marriages is the will of God in Christ concerning us. The fact that we respect God's authority over our husbands and His ability to lead, perfect, influence, and teach our husbands in all areas is the will of God in Christ Jesus concerning us. Psalms 32:8 says, "I will instruct thee and teach thee in the way which thou shalt go; I will guide thee with mine eye."

    Learning to remain silent at the right times so we both can mature spiritually, as well as, our trust in the Lord growing stronger is the will of God in Christ Jesus concerning us. Recognizing our husbands can receive from God is the will of God in Christ Jesus concerning us. We are in our individual particular situations to learn these lessons.

    Sometimes, the situations we encounter within our marriages are not things that need to be shared with our best friends or our mothers. It's at these times, also, that we must encourage ourselves in the Lord. It's at times when others would not understand or misjudge our husband that we must encourage ourselves in the Lord.

I Samuel 30:16, "They were spread abroad upon all

the earth, eating and drinking, and dancing, because of all the great spoil that they had taken out of the land of the Philistines."

After we have set things in order we'll be able to dance and rejoice because of the great spoil we and the God Head (Father, Son, and Holy Spirit) take from the enemy. Dancing is the spoil we take from the enemy. Dancing in this verse was a sign of victory and gain. Now that we know we have the victory we can gain our hearts desire. II Corinthians 2:14, "Now thanks be unto God, which always causeth us to triumph in Christ, and maketh manifest the savor of his knowledge by us in every place.

I Samuel 30:18, "And David recovered all..."

Wise women of God will recover all. Joel 2: 25, "And I will restore to you the years that the locust hath eaten." It may seem as if (locust) circumstances, attitudes, maybe even separation have eaten away the years of our marriages, but God wants us to know He will restore those years. The love will be there. The admiration will be there. The affection will be there. The private times and the special memories will all be there. This information is reiterated again.

I Samuel 30:19, "David recovered all."

Celia Wilson

This is the second time the Bible says David recovered all. We know Matthew 18:16 reads, "That in the mouth of two or three witnesses every word may be established." Wives, we must let our recovery, our restoration be established in our hearts then watch it manifest in our lives. Praise God.

I Samuel 30:20, "And David took…………………………..all the flocks and the herds, and said, this is David's spoil."

Wives, we will be able to TAKE ALL. I said TAKE ALL the enemy tried to steal from us. We'll say, "This is (insert your name here) spoil. This is what I've snatched from the devil; my precious husband and my marriage." Psalms 103:20, "Bless the Lord, ye his angels that excel in strength, that do his commandments, hearkening unto the voice of his word." The angels, the Father, Son, and Holy Spirit are all on our side. The battle is already won according to Psalms 55:18 which reads, "He hath delivered my soul in peace from the battle that was against me; for there were many with me." You are not alone in this. Wives pray and listen to the Spirit of God say, "Be still and know that I am God." Psalms 46:10. In this passage "Be Still" means – to let go, to cause to fall. Wives let go. Let go of your hold on God's Anointed Husband letting him fall right into his Heavenly Father's loving waiting arms.

Call Him

When your prayer life seems dry,
And you feel God doesn't hear,
What makes you draw nigh?
What leads you to draw near?

He said call unto me,
And I will answer thee,
And I will show thee great
And mighty things, which thou knoweth not.

You grab hold of this reality,
And you cry out and you seek.
His spirit will bring clarity,
Cause he does truly dwell with thee.

CHAPTER 3
WHAT IS A HEDGE AND HOW TO PRAY ONE FOR SOMEONE?

ANOINTED Married Christian Men

    In Smith's Bible Dictionary, "hedge" is defined this way: The Hebrew word thus rendered denotes simply that which surrounds or encloses, whether it be a stone wall (as in Proverbs 24:31 and Ezekiel 42:10) or a fence of other materials. The Random House Dictionary defines hedge this way: 1. A row of bushes or small trees forming a boundary. 2. Any barrier or boundary. 3. A protection against loss. 4. To enclose with or surround by or as by a hedge. We know a hedge is a barrier that surrounds and protects against a possible loss. The question we should ask is, "Why do we need to have a barrier around our husbands?" Another question we could ask is, "What loss are we being protected against?" Our husbands need to be surrounded by the power of prayer and the angels of God. The hedge could possibly protect us from losing our marriages, our husbands, or anything pertaining to our husbands; for instance his job, his health, his car, his dreams, and so on.

    The Bible has several examples of a hedge being put around men. In Lamentations 3:7, Jeremiah had a hedge put around him by God. The scripture reads, "He hath hedged me about, that I cannot get out: he hath made my chain heavy." We can see God is the one who put up the hedge. It is the only way one can be put up. Our prayer should be directed to God when we are praying to have a hedge placed around our husbands. The reference

Celia Wilson

to the "chain" in the latter part of the scripture brings to mind what the Apostle Paul said in Ephesians 6:20, about his being an ambassador in bonds or chains. What he said in Ephesians 3:1, about his being the prisoner of Jesus Christ correlates as well. I don't know about you, but I want my husband to be the prisoner of Jesus Christ. I want him to be surrounded - an ambassador in bonds. I want him to be surrounded so he can't get away from the Lord.

Job 3:23 reads, "Why is light given to man whose way is hid, and whom God hath hedged in?" This scripture lets us know that if God has a man hedged in He will directly illuminate his way. He will give him guidance. Husbands need to be led by the Spirit of God every second of every day. Job 1:10 reads, "Hast not thou made a hedge about him, and about his house, and about all that he hath on every side? Thou hast blessed the work of his hands and his substance is increased in the land." This is the third instance of God placing a hedge around someone. We see from this scripture, if God has a hedge around a man on every side he will be blessed at his work, as well as, in what he gains.

However, it should be pointed out that Satan asked God to remove the hedge that was around Job. God did. If you don't know what happened read the entire book of Job. Putting up a hedge is serious business. It should not be taken lightly. In Job's case his latter state was even better than the first, only because he was a faithful servant of the Lord God. Through all that Satan put him through, he remained faithful to God. When we decide to choose this course of action we must make certain we are rooted and grounded in the Word of God. We have to ensure we trust in the Lord with all our heart, soul, mind, and strength.

     Next, we will look at Ecclesiastes 10:8 which reads, "And whoso breaketh a hedge, a serpent shall bite him." This scripture could be read this way: and whoso breaks a hedge shall reap an unpleasant result. Changing your mind once you have asked God to put up a hedge is not good. Also, if husbands try doing something contrary to why the hedge was put in place something bad will probably happen. For instance, if you pray God put up a hedge around your husband so he can't get to that bar where he hangs out with the guys from work and drinks till all hours of the night wasting the family's needed finances; if he tries to do this once the hedge is up he might end up getting into a fight at the bar being charged with assault, or getting charged with being drunk and disorderly, or he might get stopped by the police on the way home for driving under the influence. Know this though, all things work together for good to those who are called according to God's purpose. (Romans 8:28) Maybe after this he'll seek help for his addiction.

Lastly, if someone causes husbands to do something contrary to the hedge we can expect some kind of bad result on their end. For instance, if a wife prays a hedge be put up around her husband so he can't get to the bookie or to his girlfriend when the husband has really made an effort to avoid these people; if they show up at the husband's job the hedge is broken. The bookie might be arrested, or his car might be towed away, or the girlfriend's job might relocate her to Miami, etc. The point is they won't be bothering that husband again.

God has not given us a Spirit of Fear. We know He will give us what we ask for. He does not play with us, especially when we are entering into spiritual warfare. A hedge is one of those weapons that can be both offensive and defensive. It is like a spiritual tank. It can protect whatever is inside, but at the same time it can attack and defend itself.

ANOINTED Married Christian Men

PRAYER FOR YOU (I)

Celia Wilson

    As an aid in the final step here is an example of a prayer to pray a hedge up around a Christian husband.

    Dear Heavenly Father, I praise You. I worship and adore You. I thank You for Your Word. I thank You for the good, perfect, anointed husband You have given to me. I ask You now according to Your Word in Matthew 7:7-11, where You say I should ask and You will give me good things. Again, in James 4:2, You say I have not because I ask not, and when I ask, I ask amiss.

    I'm asking You Father to put up a hedge around my husband (insert his name). I pray he be blessed according to III John 2, where You say, Beloved, I wish above all things that you prosper and be in health, even as thy soul prospers. Let my husband's soul prosper more than I could ever hope or think, Lord. I pray, Father, that (insert husband's name) will not be able to get out of the hedge to do "his thing" if it is negative, unhealthy, or against Your Will, and if "his thing" does not coincide with Your Will for him according to Psalms 37:23, The steps of a good man (insert his name) are ordered by the Lord: and he (insert his name) delighted in his way." Also, according to Proverbs 16:9, "A man's (insert his name) heart plans his way, but the Lord directs his (insert his name) steps."

    Father, thank you for conforming his will to

ANOINTED Married Christian Men

Your way in Jesus' Precious Name. According to Psalms 119:133, "Order (insert husband's name) steps in thy word; and let not any iniquity have dominion over (insert his name)." Lord, I also pray (insert husband's name) will do the Will of You who sent him according to John 6:38.

 Father, in the Name of Jesus I bind every principality, every power, every ruler of the darkness of this world, all spiritual wickedness in high places from having any influence over (insert his name) to try and break this hedge according to Ephesians 6:12 and Matthew 12:29, "Or else how can one (insert your name) enter into a strong man's house and spoil his goods except he (insert your name) bind the strong man? And then he (insert your name) will spoil his house." And Matthew 16:19, "And I will give unto thee (insert both your names) the keys of the kingdom of heaven and whatsoever thou (enter your name) shalt loose on earth shall be loosed in heaven." I pray selfishness, abusive speech and actions, inconsiderateness, lack of attention, lack of sexual passion for me, neglect, ill manners, stress, tension, worry, lack of drive and focus, illiteracy, laziness, underemployment, self-hate, lack of self-worth, and any other hindrances be loosed from (insert his name).

 In Jesus' Name I pray and I thank You for You are faithful who promised. You watch over Your Word to perform it. Your Word does not return unto

Celia Wilson

You void, but it accomplishes that which You please, and it prospers in the thing (insert his name) whereto You sent it. I know, God, that You are not a man that You should lie. I realize and have confidence in Your Word that is why I'm calling those things that be not as though they were. I count it done and expect positive results in the mighty name of Jesus Christ our Lord. Strengthen me in Jesus', Amen.

CHAPTER 4
HOW TO PLEAD
THE BLOOD OF JESUS

Celia Wilson

Before we can begin to plead the Blood of Jesus we must first know what "plead" means and we must understand what Jesus' Blood does for us. The word "plead" is defined as: 1. An appeal or earnest request. 2. To put forward a plea in court: 4. To make a plea of a specific kind.

When we plead the Blood of Jesus we are making an appeal or earnest request to God on behalf of or because of the Blood that Jesus shed for us. The reason the plea is in a court room setting will be brought out later in the study. Our plea is specific because it is the Blood of Jesus. His Blood is our plea.

The word "plea" is defined as a defendant's answer to a charge. We are the defendants. We are answering the charge of our accuser, the devil. Revelations 12:10 reads, "And I heard a loud voice saying in heaven, Now is come salvation, and strength, and the kingdom of our God, and the power of his Christ: FOR THE ACCUSER OF OUR BRETHREN IS CAST DOWN, WHICH ACCUSED THEM BEFORE OUR GOD DAY AND NIGHT," Try to picture this scene in heaven. God is the judge on His throne in the middle of the courtroom. Satan is on the left side of God accusing us of all sorts of crimes against God. Jesus is on the right side of God pointing to his own blood stained hands, feet, head, and back each time the devil accuses us of something. We are standing right in front of God who is saying Isaiah 42:

26, "Put me in remembrance: let us plead together: declare thou, that thou mayest be justified." O.K. the devil accuses us on one hand and Jesus says I've got it covered on the other. God tells us to remind Him of what His Son's Blood did for us, to speak out, to report to Him. He invites us to talk about this with Him so we can identify with our being justified.

    Someone can tell us we are rich, but if we start trying to spend money like millionaires we'll end up in serious trouble. If, however, we sit down with the banker, the lawyer, and the accountant to go over all the figures to find out who gave us the money and how much we actually have then we can begin to spend like millionaires, because we'll know exactly how much we have. It is the same way with all the benefits we'll obtain as we plead Jesus' Blood together with God and as we study to find out what benefits we actually have in Jesus' Blood.

    Let's look at a picture of the devil accusing us before God.

> Job 1:6-12, Now there was a day when the sons of God (angels) came to present themselves before the Lord, and Satan came also among them. And the Lord said unto Satan, Whence cometh thou? Then Satan answered the Lord, and said, from going to and fro in the earth, and from walking up and down in it. And the Lord said unto Satan, Hast thou considered my servant Job, that

Celia Wilson

> there is none like him in the earth, a perfect and an upright man, one that feareth God and escheweth (avoids) evil? Then Satan answered the Lord, and said, Doth Job fear God for nothing? Hast not thou made a hedge about him and about his house, and about all that he hath on every side? Thou hast blessed the work of his hands, and his substance is increased in the land. But put forth thine hand now, and touch all that he hath, and he (Job) will curse thee (God) to thy face. And the Lord said unto Satan, Behold, all that he hath is in thy power; only upon himself, put not forth thine hand. So Satan went forth from the presence of the Lord.
> Words in parentheses are my insertion.

God was telling Satan how good Job was. Satan says sure, God, I bet if you stop blessing him he'll curse you to your face. Who wouldn't be a good man if he had everything handed to him by God? In essence Satan accused Job of being a user, of being an insincere servant who only worshipped God because of the benefits. What an accusation.

Then we see in Daniel 10:2-3 that Daniel is praying and fasting. In verse 12 the angel who was sent to bring the answer to his prayer says, "Fear not Daniel, for from the first day thou didst set thine heart to understand and to chasten thyself before thy God, thy WORDS were heard, and I am come FOR THY WORDS. Verse 13 reads, but the princes of the kingdom of Persia withstood me one and twenty days: but, lo, Michael, one of the chief princes came to help me: and I remained there with the king of Persia." The angel mentioned this fact twice that Daniel's words are what brought him. In Psalms 35: 5-6 the scriptures read, "Plead my cause, O Lord, strive with them that strive with me: fight against them that fight against me. Let them be as chaff before the wind: and let the angel of the Lord chase them." Speaking "Jesus' Blood" out loud brings our Lord on the scene. He is the Captain of the Heavenly Host so they obey His Word. Once His Word is spoken His angels get to work on our behalf.

Psalms 9:12 says, "When he maketh inquisition for blood he remembereth them (us): he forgetteth not the cry of the humble." Word in parentheses is my insertion. Our Lord makes inquisition or official investigations into who we are, into who is covered by the blood and how, into whom is interceding on behalf of whom. He does this when we are accused by Satan or when we speak forth His Blood. The angels of the Lord only heed His voice, His WORD. They take pleasure in helping fulfill His WORD as it's spoken. Jesus is not the only one who can speak His WORD. When we confess the Word of God, the angels move. Praise God.

Psalms 103:19-21 reads,

Celia Wilson

> The Lord hath prepared his throne in the heavens; and his kingdom ruleth over all. Bless the Lord, ye his angels that excel in strength, that do his commandments, hearkening unto the voice of His WORD. Bless ye the Lord, all ye his hosts, ye ministers of his that do his pleasure.

We are the voice of His WORD when we open our mouths and say what the Word says.

Now that we know we are suppose to and that we can plead the Blood of Jesus we need to know if we can plead His Blood for our good, perfect, anointed husbands. Intercession is a vital part of God's perfect plan. Intercession is a prayer to God as we represent someone else. God started intercession. In Ezekiel 22:30 God is speaking, "And I sought for a man among them that should make up the hedge, and stand in the gap before me for the land, that I should not destroy it; but I found none." Praise God. There are many facts in this scripture that will benefit and enlighten us.

God searched among all the men of the earth finding all of them to be under sin. He wanted a man to make a hedge or make up the hedge for mankind. He wanted a man to be mankind's protection against loss; to be the fortress that surrounds humankind. God wanted a man who would stand in the gap to become the bridge connecting (sinful) man back to

ANOINTED Married Christian Men

Himself. In the earth he found no such man. Isaiah 59:16, "And he saw that there was no man, and wondered that there was no intercessor; therefore his arm brought salvation unto him: and his righteousness, it sustained him." Jesus was the arm of God who brought our salvation to God. Psalms 40:7, "Then said I (Jesus) my insertion, lo, I come in the volume of the book it is written of me." Jesus knew His destiny was to come intercede for humans with his life by shedding His Blood. His coming is predicted and prophesied throughout the Hebrew Scriptures, which is referred to as "the book" in this verse of scripture. (A note on Praying a Hedge: Jesus is the HEDGE God puts around our husbands or anyone else we pray for. I have not seen in any other scripture where God refers to any other person as a HEDGE.)

      Then, in Isaiah 6:8, Isaiah is having a vision. In it he hears the voice of the Lord God saying, "Whom shall I send, and who will go for US? Then said I (Isaiah) my insertion, Here am I, send me." In this scripture Isaiah is a type of Christ. We also need to understand that the word "Lord" means "Adonai or My lords". Notice the plural of the word "lords." We often say Lord God in reference to God and Jesus is Lord when talking about Jesus. Similarly, when God refers to "us" in Heaven He is referring to Himself, Jesus, and the Holy Spirit. Remember He used the same word in Genesis when He said, "Let us make

Celia Wilson

man in our image." This unity of the three is known as the "Trinity". So this is a spiritual conversation between God, His Son, and the Holy Spirit. First, God says, "Whom shall I send?" Next, the Holy Spirit says, "Who will go for (US)?" Lastly, Jesus answers, "Here am I, send me." God did send Jesus in the form of a man to take away the sins of the world. Praise God. Jesus is still interceding for us. In Hebrews 7:25 we read, "Wherefore he (Jesus) is able also to save them to the uttermost that come unto God by him, seeing he ever liveth to make intercession for them." Word in parentheses is my insertion. We also know through scripture that the Holy Spirit has a part in intercession.

> Romans 8:26-27 reads, Likewise the Spirit also helpeth our infirmities: for we know not what to pray for as we ought; but the Spirit itself maketh intercession for us with groaning which cannot be uttered. And he (God) that searcheth the hearts knoweth what is the mind of the spirit (of man), because he (Holy Spirit) maketh intercession for the saints according to the will of God.
> Words in parentheses are my insertion.

So far we know God indeed started

intercession. Jesus interceded, still intercedes today as does the Holy Spirit. Some may say those are spiritual holy beings. None of them are just ordinary people like we are. We will look at some everyday people who intercede. Hebrews 2:18 reads, "For in that he himself hath suffered being tempted, he is able to succor (help) them that are tempted." Word in parentheses is my insertion. This scripture is about Jesus. That's right, Jesus suffered through temptation, just as we do, but since He did not sin He was able to intercede for us with the sacrifice of his body. In His humanity He was just an ordinary person like you and me. He interceded.

    Genesis 18:20-32, allows us to look at Abraham as he interceded before God for the cities of Sodom and Gomorrah. God had promised not to destroy those cities if He could find 10 righteous men living in them. This came about because Abraham interceded. At first God was just going to take the cities out, but he changed His mind saying O.K., I'll be cool, Abraham, if I can find 10 righteous men just because you asked. He couldn't find 10 though.

    In Colossians 4:12 Paul writes about a man named, Ep' –a-phras, who is a Christian that (always) labors fervently for you in prayers. That LABOR or PRAYER WORK is INTERCESSION. Praise God that intercession can render positive results to those for whom we pray. Those are just some of the examples of regular Christian people like you and me who interceded for others. These scriptures let us know we can intercede for our Good, Perfect, Anointed Husbands.

We know Jesus shed His Blood to save us, but His Blood provides us with many more things. When we plead His Blood over our husbands it helps to know all the areas that will be covered. Jesus shed His Blood to cover our sin. I John 1:17, "...the blood of Jesus Christ his Son cleanseth us from all sin." Revelations 1:15, "Unto him that loved us, and washed us from our sins in his own blood." So, when we plead His Blood over our husbands they are clean spiritually. We must say they are clean.

When we pray or intercede we need to have a clear picture of how Jesus' Blood covers our men. The word "cover" is defined as: 1. To place something over or upon. 2. To shelter or protect, to hide from view. 3. To include, deal with, or provide for. 4. To insure against risk or loss. 5. To provide an alibi for.

Point number one is Jesus placed His Blood over or upon each and every born-again husband. From this point on it is understood that a man is no longer seen as just a man in his natural state, but he is seen as a man covered with the Blood of Jesus. God doesn't see just a man when He looks at a man covered with Jesus' Blood. He sees a precious, priceless, valuable man. As wives we have to see the big picture.

The second point is Jesus' Blood shelters or

protects; it hides our husbands from view. Jesus' Blood is a tangible place in which to dwell, in the spiritual realm. Once our men are in it they are protected from the attacks of the enemy. This does not mean they won't be attacked.

Then we read that our husbands are hidden from view by the Blood of Jesus. Whose view are they hidden from? Well, first they are hidden from God's view. Our Heavenly Father sees Jesus now when He looks at those men. He does not see just a natural man. Praise God. He sees a natural man filled with supernatural possibility due to the covering. It's like an ice cream cone dipped in that hard chocolate shell.

Next, they are hidden from demonic view. Satan is a fallen angel who can only be in one place at one time. His demons are fallen angels, also, who are sent to do Satan's will, which is to kill, steal, and destroy. There are different levels of demonic authority according to Ephesians 6:12. There are principalities, powers, rulers of the darkness of this world, and spiritual wickedness in high places of authority. Satan has given them all certain tasks in certain places, at certain times, towards certain families and people.

For instance, if some demonic spirits of theft were sent to your husband's family you'd know. How? Because his great-grandfather, his grandfather, his father, his uncle, his sister, and he

Celia Wilson

will all be thieves. Stealing will run in the family or those demons will run throughout the family. Those demons will follow him. Even after he is saved they will try to oppress him. If you plead the Blood of Jesus over your husband the demons won't recognize him as Paul the thief. No, all they will see is Jesus' Blood covering the form of a man. They can't attack Jesus' Blood. So what happens? Eventually, they leave, go back to their boss (the Devil) and say, "Hey, we can't find that guy, Paul, anymore. The Blood of Jesus is all in the way. Can we have another assignment?" Then their boss says, "O.K., all of you can have new assignments, but one of you go back there and wait. Maybe if you cause enough havoc and disorder in that home, in that family you can get a glimpse of Paul. If you do see him, hit him and hit him hard." So wives this means we have got to pray without ceasing, I Thess. 5:17. We have to be instant in season and out of season, II Timothy 4:2. The word "instant" in this verse means to place upon. This means wives are suppose to place the Blood of Jesus upon their husbands every day, even when things are going great, to ensure they continue going great.

  The third point of cover, as it pertains to Jesus' blood, is that in His Blood our husbands are included, dealt with, and provided for. Praise God. When we plead the Blood of Jesus before the Father it allows the Holy Spirit to minister to our husbands,

ANOINTED Married Christian Men

because all the forces and circumstances that were hindering him from hearing and receiving from the Holy Spirit are kept away by the Blood. Also, because these men are covered with Jesus' Blood they are included in the heavenly family, counted as sons of the Most High God according to Romans 8:14-16. Since Christian husbands are included as part of God's family through Jesus' Blood they are also provided for as Romans 8:17 tells us. What do they receive as a result of being a joint-heir with Christ? Everything Jesus has. It can be summed up in one word, VICTORY. When husbands are victorious wives definitely have victory. Why? Because all the contention, stress, occasion to deviate from faith and peace is gone. Together in victory they can combat all the other issues they'll face in life and win.

    The Blood of Jesus insulates husbands against risk or loss. We don't have to be concerned about the risk they are in at work, or while driving, or ministering, or while they are engaged in any of life's normal activities. Jesus' Blood is like their spiritual bodyguard. Since they are covered with "The Blood" Satan's assignments to kill, steal, or destroy are thwarted.

    Another really good point is the Blood of Jesus provides an alibi for our husbands, God's men. Therefore, when the accuser starts to lie to God, Jesus says to God, "Excuse me, Father, I have this man covered. If you look at him you'll see MY

BLOOD." Oh, if wives could get this picture. It is not easy realizing that our husbands have an alibi after they've gotten on our nerves, seriously. It is going to take a lot of prayer and mental training to see Jesus' Blood instead of someone we want to shake.

Now that we understand all the areas Jesus' Blood covers we must move on to another essential area. In order to plead the Blood of Jesus we must have faith in His Blood. Romans 3:25 reads, "Whom God hath set forth to be a propitiation (a mercy seat or place where we gain favor) through faith in His Blood, to declare his righteousness for the remission of sins that are past, through the forbearance of God." Words in parentheses are my insertion. We must believe the only reason Jesus is our husband's mercy seat or place where they gain favor is because of the Blood Jesus poured out on Calvary. We must have faith. Our faith is a substantive entity. It is an actual substance. Jesus' Blood is substantive, too. In the spiritual realm when added together these two substances equal positive substance in the lives of the men we love. Remember this equation when negativity tries to come in to deter your thinking. +FAITH + +JESUS' BLOOD = +GOOD, PERFECT, ANOINTED HUSBAND. Amen.

"And almost all things are by the law purged with blood; and without shedding of blood is no remission." Hebrews 9:22. The word "purged" means cleansed and "remission" means sending

ANOINTED Married Christian Men

away. The above scripture paraphrased would read: And almost all things are cleansed with blood in the law; and without bloodshed no sin is sent away. This is how things were cleansed in biblical times; with the sacrificial blood of animals. God cleansed us the same way. He let Jesus die and shed His Blood to cleanse us from all sin and to present us holy and acceptable unto our God.

In the following paragraphs we will find out some of the specific areas in the lives of our husbands and ourselves cleansed by the shedding of Jesus' precious Blood. Hebrews 9:14 lets us know His Blood purged our conscience from dead works. The scripture reads, "How much more shall the blood of Christ, who through the eternal Spirit offered himself without spot to God, purge your conscience from dead works to serve the living God?" Christian wives have had their conscious cleansed from remembering past mistakes, past arguments, past unhealthy feelings, and past disappointments. Remembering all these things will only lead to dead works. Remembering the stuff is a dead work in and of itself. Why? Because bringing up past unpleasantness will cause new arguments, mistakes, disappointments, and bad feelings. The Bible reads, "Be not deceived: evil communication corrupts good manners." (Corinthians 15:33) As wives we have to watch what we say. Also, we have to make sure we don't provoke our husbands to produce evil

Celia Wilson

communications.

> Ephesians 5:26, 29, 31, 32, Be ye angry, and sin not: let not the sun go down upon your wrath: Let no corrupt communication proceed out of your mouth, but that which is good to the use of edifying, that it may minister grace unto the hearers. Let all bitterness, and wrath, and anger, and clamor, and evil speaking be put away from you, with all malice. And be ye kind one to another, tenderhearted, forgiving one another, even as God for Christ's sake hath for given you.

So, as we begin to plead the Blood of Jesus daily, remember the enemy will come to test us to see if we really have faith in what Jesus' Blood can do and has done. When we allow ourselves to be upset because of our husbands or we become angry sinning is not necessary. Saying the first thing that pops into our minds is not necessary. Stopping, praying - then saying something tenderly to him, or something kind, or positive would be better. If it really is hard to say something tenderly to him and it's even harder to be quiet, just say The Blood, The

ANOINTED Married Christian Men

Blood, The Blood of Jesus, over and over again out loud. They may look at us strangely, or their speech may get louder but watch how they leave us alone. Once the quiet sets in, that Blood will begin to cleanse all the harsh outside world from his spirit and mind. Once the quiet sets in, God's Good, Perfect, Anointed husband will succumb to the Lord's graciousness as he interacts with his wife.

  Notice that we are supposed to SAY, The Blood of Jesus over and over. We are not suppose to SCREAM it, YELL it, or HOLLER it. We are calling on our Savior to help us maintain our composure. We are pleading with God to allow some of our mate's good qualities to surface and that we'll recognize them. We are not cursing him with Jesus' Blood, so we have to be cognizant of the tone in which we speak.

> Finally, brethren (or sisteren),
> whatsoever things are true,
> whatsoever things are honest,
> whatsoever things are just,
> whatsoever things are pure,
> whatsoever things are lovely,
> whatsoever things are of good report;
> if there be any virtue, and if there be
> any praise; think on these things,
> Philippians 4:8
>
> Words in parentheses are my insertion.

Celia Wilson

If we can keep a positive attitude and disposition our husbands might, too. Can we visualize our husbands grabbing our hand and saying, "Baby, let's pray."? Can we visualize him praying for our kids, first, when they start to have a physical challenge? Can we picture him turning off the T.V. opting to read and study the Word? If we can then we allow God's Will to manifest it in his life. Why? Because Galatians 6:9 says in the Amplified Bible, "And let us (wives) not lose heart and grow weary and faint in acting nobly and doing right, for in due season we shall reap, if we do not loosen and relax our courage, and faint." Word in parentheses is my insertion. If we don't get fed up, tired, and nonchalant about the way we treat God's men, God will reward us with a great harvest. Can't you see it? A harvest of Holy Spirit filled, tongue talking, miracle working, devoted, sensitive, caring husbands.

We have to draw upon the fruit the Holy Spirit has placed within us. We have loving spirits, not warring spirits; at least we should with our husbands. We have joyous spirits, not depressed defeated spirits. Our spirits are peaceful, not anxious. Our spirits are long-suffering, instead of non-suffering. We have gentle spirits, not cold, hard, non-compromising spirits. We have good spirits, not bad spirits. Our spirits are faithful, not fearful. Our spirits are meek, not haughty.

Jesus' Blood has provided us with

redemption. Our husbands have this same redemption. Ephesians 1:7 reads, "In whom we have redemption through his blood, the forgiveness of sins, according to the riches of his grace." Hebrews 9:12 says, "Neither by the blood of goats and calves, but by his own blood he entered in once into the holy place, having obtained eternal redemption for us." Redemption is defined as: 1. The act of redeeming or state of being redeemed. 2. Deliverance from sin. Redeem means: 1. To buy back. 2. To buy or pay off. 3. To exchange. 4. To discharge or fulfill. 6. To obtain the release of, as by paying ransom. 7. To set free or save, as a sinner.

    Jesus' Blood provided us with redemption from sin before we were born. When we plead His Blood over our men what exactly will our husbands receive redemption from? They will be redeemed from anything contrary to God's Word in their lives. As long as we are pleading the Blood they will be in a constant state of being redeemed. They will be placed in a spiritual place where they can receive spiritual operations from God as we intercede for them.

    This is possible because Jesus has brought back all the good, perfect, anointed things about God's men from the devil. He paid off the debt our marriages and relationships would have had to pay as a result of the disharmony and disunity that was created. Therefore, we can't use statements like this as a reason or excuse to get a divorce: "I just can't

Celia Wilson

live with him anymore." Some wives say God said our marriages had to flow decently and in order since our marriage is not in order I don't have to remain married. If our marriages are not in order we can't blame our mates until we have checked ourselves. Some women keep many a squabble going.

Christian women have to really understand that the little things our husbands do to tick us off should not cause strife in a marriage. They won't cause strife unless we let them. If we recognize it (whatever it is he does or says) as a match to start the fire of strife (within us) we have the power in our mouths to blow it out, right? Before anything is burned we reach out our hands and snuff that fire out. It might sting a little bit, initially, but with practice we become more skillful at averting that trap. Inwardly we can say something like, "Oh, I see what this is, the devil is a liar. I won't allow those words or actions to ignite strife within me." Then say something like this aloud, "Oh, Honey I love you so much. Thank you for your insight. I'm so glad God blessed me with you to cover me. I'll be back." We can then exit the room quickly to pray or take a deep breath, if needed.

Jesus exchanged Himself, His Blood, for that of Christian husbands. This means spiritually these men have Jesus' Blood running through their veins. Satan could care less about some lost sinner man, but, because Jesus has exchanged His own body and blood for that of God's men, Satan cares a great deal. He comes at them with all he's got. If all the men have is a wife who is looking to place blame on him he surely will be easy prey. Realize this: to Satan these men represent some of Jesus. Their downfall is of great price to him.

> Forasmuch, as ye know that ye were not redeemed with corruptible things as silver and gold, from your aimless conduct received by tradition from your fathers, but with the precious Blood of Christ, as of a lamb without blemish and without spot. I Peter 1: 18-19.

It doesn't matter what happened in our parent's marriage or how our mothers treated our fathers. It doesn't matter what we've been taught to believe about men---all men. The precious Blood of Christ will present our husbands to us as lambs without blemish or spot. The enemy would love to slaughter our Godly men, but they have so many spiritual bodyguards that he can't. Wives are the closest bodyguards our husbands have in the natural or physical realm.

Jesus also discharged or fulfilled every pain, affliction, and temper flare up. Every arena that Satan would have our husbands perform in has been closed. Jesus has already played those parts winning the Oscar and Tony Awards. He not only won the awards, He took all categories, Best Man, Best Supporting Man, Best Stand In, and Best Director. Praise God. So we can rest in the fact that it is God's responsibility to heal and calm our husband's spirits and emotions. As Christian women we must forget the lies the enemy tells us like, "If you pray for him he'll act worse." or "Your kids are going to be just as stubborn and ignorant as he is." or "All he's really interested in is your body. You see he never listens to you or talks to you. He never listens to your advice." We know Satan tells lies to make us think and believe we are in some kind of never ending nightmare cycle. Wrong. Jesus, by His Blood has obtained the release of our husbands, our husband's children, and anyone else in relationship with them, including us. Yes, Jesus paid the ransom our blood never could.

As a result of all this God's men are free. Their marriages are saved. We can believe God for a harmonious, over-coming, over flowing married life. The more we plead Jesus' Blood the freer our men will be. Their initial freedom might be they verbally share some things we'd wish they wouldn't. For instance, they want us to lose weight, or they wish we'd stay off the telephone, or they don't like our new hairstyle. Don't look at these things as criticism. Instead view them as a beginning in their process of learning how to freely express their thoughts, emotions, desires, needs, and goals. Really, many men have not had a lot of experience in this area. Some have and that's good, but for those who have not wouldn't helping them be a loving Christian gesture?

Once initial progress is made God can expand them into areas like, "Honey, I think we should pray together more." Or "Darling, have you ever noticed this before in this passage of scripture?" Or "Bay, what are you doing today, can we spend some time together?" If we come along telling our husbands to be quiet {when they (as little babies) begin to express things that use to be impossible for them to verbalize} we stifle all the new exciting things they have to share with us. It is like when a baby is learning to talk. First, it babbles all the time in a language we can't understand, sometimes when it's inappropriate. We don't start talking to the infant in the same language (you know that goo goo ga ga stuff) in which he is speaking. No, sometimes we change the setting or just let the baby finish. We always continue speaking correct English so the baby will eventually learn to speak English. It's the same way with a man who is beginning to discover he can express those things deep inside himself which he's kept locked inside for years. Anyway, some of us do need to lose weight just to get/stay healthy, some of us talk on the phone way too much, and changing our hairstyle is not major, though it might be expensive or time consuming.

Colossians 1:14 reads, "In whom we have redemption through his blood, even the forgiveness of sins." Remember our husbands have their redemption through Jesus' Blood, so even their sins are forgiven. As we plead Christ's Blood over them we will begin to have a forgiving heart, just as Christ does. When Jesus forgives He forgets and we just might begin to forgive even if we can't forget. Trust God.

Romans 5:9, lets us know this, "Being now justified by His Blood, we shall be saved from wrath through him." Not only does Jesus redeem us with His Blood, He also justifies us. Justified is defined as; 1. To show to be justified or right. 3. To absolve of guilt. These definitions are pretty clear. Since God sees Jesus' Blood when He looks at our husbands, naturally they are shown to be right. Why? Because II Corinthians 5:21 reads, "For he hath made him to be sin for us who knew no sin; that we might be made the righteousness of God in him." Jesus did not sin. He became sin for our men. He became sin for all of us. In so doing He has made us the righteousness of God. The fact stands whether we think it does or not; whether our husbands act like it or not. How dare we attack, mistreat, accuse, or misuse the righteousness of God in Christ Jesus.

The Blood benefits us in that our men have grace and peace with God. In Romans 5:20 we read,

ANOINTED Married Christian Men

"That as sin hath reigned unto death even so might grace reign through righteousness unto eternal life by Jesus Christ our Lord." Grace is simply being in God's favor. Our husbands are in God's favor not because of anything they have done, but because of what Jesus did. Remember **that** when we pray and plead the Blood over them. They should not have to earn our prayers of support. We should be gracious enough to give them willingly.

Colossians 1:20 says, "And having made peace through the blood of his cross, by him to reconcile all things to himself; by him, whether they be things in earth, or things in heaven." Women, you have peace no matter what the circumstances say. Having peace means not having war. We should make an agreement with ourselves and our spouses to end any sign of war that may be present in our lives. Peace is a state of harmony between a husband and wife. The Bible says a house divided against itself, won't stand. (Matt. 12:25) When we start focusing on the areas of harmony in our lives the areas of disharmony will slowly start to diminish. Peace is the freedom from normal disorder. As Christians we don't operate under normal circumstances. We operate in supernatural circumstances.

Consequently, we should not accept any disorder as "normal" disorder. Our Father is not the author of confusion. We can believe this: where there is disorder there is confusion. We can't accept any in our marriages and most of all we mustn't bring any confusion home. Peace is having a mind free from fear, anxiety, or annoyance. Praise God. Praise Jesus for His Blood. Jesus' Blood ensures that our husbands should not be fearful of our over-spending while he is out working. It ensures husbands will have no anxiety in their lives as a result of their wives behavior. Sure he will run into situations on the job, or while he is outside the home, but when he comes home he should find relaxation, support, praise, love, admiration, and respect. Husbands are freed from having annoying wives. Proverbs 21:19, "Better to dwell in the wilderness, than with a contentious and angry wife." and Proverbs 21:9 reads, "Better to dwell in a corner of a housetop, than in a house shared with a contentious woman." We can certainly ensure our husbands prefer being with us as opposed to dwelling in the wilderness or on the roof because our disposition makes living with us so unbearable. So understand as we plead the Blood over our husbands we are pleading that "we" stop being an annoyance to him, as well. We won't pick, complain, or be critical. We'll be a pleasure to be around.

      Peace is silence or stillness. Husbands deserve some peace and quiet to hear from the Holy Spirit. They don't need us in their ear telling them "Huh, you're supposed to be the spiritual head of our family and you never pray. God is not directing a single step you make and you expect me to follow and obey you. You must be kidding." No, wives, we are kidding ourselves. If we would leave our men alone sometime, maybe they could hear the voice of God. Let them have some "me" time. Give them and the Holy Spirit a chance to be alone together without interfering with their ability to receive from the Lord. Jesus' Blood will fix this area, also. Now, watch how Colossians 1:21:22 reads paraphrased to fit our topic. And (your husband) that (was) sometimes alienated and (an enemy) in (his) mind by wicked works, yet now hath (Jesus) reconciled in the body of His flesh through death, to present (your husband) holy, un-blamable and un-reprovable in his sight. Pleading Jesus' Blood will cause us to have husbands who are holy, un-blamable, and un-reprovable in Jesus' sight.

     As we come to the end of this chapter we need to know one very important fact. That is Jesus' Blood makes us OVER-COMERS. We overcome sickness. We overcome physical sickness, emotional sickness, and spiritual sickness, as well. Yes, negativity is a sickness. Obsessive insecurity is a sickness. All those feelings which cause us to lash out at our husbands for no apparent reason are signs of some form of one of these sicknesses. "But he was wounded for our transgressions, he was bruised for our iniquities; the chastisement of our peace was upon him; and with his stripes we are healed", Isaiah

Celia Wilson

53:5. We are healed by our Lord's Blood as are our husbands. "Who his own self bare our sins in his own body on the tree that we, being dead to sins, should live unto righteousness; by whose stripes ye were healed", I Peter 2:24. Healing was made possible by Jesus' Blood. Our husbands will want to live righteously if they are not being constantly harassed by an un-giving, uncaring, unloving wife. His healing may come in the form of a bad habit being dropped. For instance, smoking, cursing, drinking, sitting in front of the T.V., P.C., or video game all evening, overeating, and procrastinating (wasting time). A sign that will follow will be that their relationship with the Lord will grow. It might not look like what we expect or want, but it's not up to us since we are not in charge of their spirits. The manner in which they treat and talk with their wives will change for the better, also.

      Revelations 12:11 reads, "And they overcame him by the blood of the lamb and by the word of their testimony: and they loved not their lives unto the death." Christian marriages will overcome all the devices of the devil if the couple is pleading Christ's Blood in prayer. If their testimony is based on what the Word says and if they are not focusing on their own wants and desires, but on the wants and desires of their mates, they will overcome. It doesn't matter if our husbands are not doing it or doesn't do it all the time. If we are faithful, steadfast, and consistent

ANOINTED Married Christian Men

God will grant the increase in our Good, Perfect Anointed husbands.

In the real world things happen. People get upset. Heck, stuff happens, but as women of faith we can face these issues realistically, while at the same time being the helpmeets God created us to be. We don't have to ignore or endure bad behavior because we have the wisdom and power to teach and correct our husbands (in Love) regarding those things that hurt us. Trust God.

Celia Wilson

PRAYER FOR YOU (II)

ANOINTED Married Christian Men

Before we can pray to plead the Blood of Jesus over our husbands, we need to pray His Blood over ourselves.

Dear Heavenly Father, I praise Your name. I thank You for the Blood of Jesus Christ, Your Son. I thank You that even now His Blood is cleansing me of any and all iniquity. I thank You, Father, that I no longer perform dead works, instead I work Your Word and Your work in my marriage. I plead Jesus' Blood over my attitudes, moods, and feelings. I plead His Blood over my entire mind, spirit, and body. I will no longer be a hindrance or an annoyance to my husband, but I will be the blessed helpmeet You intended me to be.

I thank You, Lord God, that with the Power of Jesus' Blood and with His eyes I will no longer see my husband with my natural eyes, but I will see him as the Good, Perfect, Anointed husband You cause him to be.

Father, help me to learn how to meet my needs (physical, emotional, spiritual, financial, intellectual, social, and creative) in positive ways without expecting my husband to meet them all for me. You said You would supply all my need, according to Your riches in glory. So I put my need in Your hands for You to meet, not the man You gave me. Cover my needs in Your Blood, Dear Jesus.

By Jesus' Blood I will be a source of peace,

Celia Wilson

gentleness, understanding, joy, and love for my husband. Father, I plead Jesus' Blood as a source of protection and deliverance from the devices of the devil. Jesus' Blood defeated you Satan. Jesus' Blood covers me and all things concerning me, therefore, I have defeated you also, Satan.

Thank You, Father, for the victory. Thank You, Lord, for causing me to be a Victorious Wife. Praise Your Holy Name in Jesus' Name, Amen.

ANOINTED Married Christian Men

PLEADING THE BLOOD OF JESUS OVER YOUR HUSBAND

Satan, right now I let you know <u>husband's name</u> is covered with the Blood of Jesus. Satan and all you demons in Hell, I bind you in the Name of Jesus because the Word of God says whatever I bind on earth shall be bound in heaven. I possess the keys to your gate. You are my enemy and I lock you out of my marriage and away from my husband. So I bind you and I loose you from <u>husband's name</u> and our marriage. You have no place here. Your accusations about my husband are a lie because of the precious shed Blood of Jesus Christ my Lord and Savior and my husband's Lord and Savior. You are cast down in the name of Jesus.

Father God, I put You in remembrance that <u>husband's name</u> is Your son and covered with Jesus' Blood. You put him in the position of being my husband. He is Your child and Your responsibility. Your Word says in Psalms 1:1-3 that blessed is <u>husband's name</u> that walketh not in the counsel of the ungodly, nor standeth in the seat of the scornful, but <u>husband's name</u> delights in the law of the Lord, and in Your law does <u>husband's name</u> meditate day and night. He shall be like a tree planted by the rivers of water, that brings forth his fruit in his season; <u>husband's name</u> leaf also shall not wither; and whatsoever <u>husband's name</u> does shall prosper. Ministering spirits be loosed in the Name of Jesus to cause all those things that Jesus Blood covers to come into <u>husband's name</u> life. I thank You, Lord, that any sin of husband's name is covered by Jesus' Blood. I thank you Father that husband's name is cleansed from any sin. I thank You Lord that all satanic assignments are broken over and concerning husband's name because of Jesus' Blood. I thank You Father that husband's name has been provided for by the Blood of Jesus.

Husband's name no longer has a conscience of dead works, but he works the works of You, Father, who have sent him. Husband's name has been redeemed through Jesus' Blood. He will always be redeemed, delivered, and the servant of only one Master. You are that Master, Heavenly Father. Father, Jesus' Blood makes husband's name free to seek and serve You, Lord, the only wise and living God.

I thank You Lord that husband's name is justified by the Blood of Jesus. Husband's Name is right and righteousness just as Jesus is. I thank You that husband's name abounds in grace and peace. He is a gracious husband and father. He has no anxiety, fear, confusion, nor annoyances. He is not warring against me, his wife, but he is ever ready to battle the enemy in Your strength and armor, Father. I thank You, Father, that husband's name has come in agreement with Your Word concerning our marriage and does not operate in disorder, nor does he cause it in Jesus' Precious Name, Amen.

CHAPTER 5
WHEN TO SEEK PROFESSIONAL ASSISTANCE

This chapter is dedicated in honor and memory of (Dr.) Tonya L. Hunter, MSSA, LSW, LIMFT, LICDC, SAP my friend, mentor, and sister in Christ whose life was tragically taken by her abusive Christian husband on 7/25/2010.

An Advocate With The Father

We are not sinless,
But we do sin less.
We are not fault free,
But we are set free.
We have an advocate with the Father
When we do wrong,
To stand on our behalf and say,
Father, I've paid for it all.

National Library of Poetry Award Winner

Celia Wilson

Malachi 2:14-16, Yet you ask, why does He reject it (your offering)? Because the Lord was witness {to the covenant made at your marriage} between you and the wife of your youth, against whom you have dealt treacherously and to whom you were faithless. Yet she is your companion and the wife of your covenant {made by your marriage vows}. And did not God make {you and your wife} one {flesh}? Did not One make you and preserve your spirit alive? And why did God make you two one? Because He sought a godly offspring {from your union}. Therefore take heed to yourself, and let no one deal treacherously and be faithless to the wife of his youth. For the Lord, the God of Israel says: I hate divorce and martial separation, and him who covers his garment {his wife} with violence. Therefore keep a watch upon your spirit {that it may be controlled by My Spirit}, that you deal not treacherously and faithlessly {with your marriage mate}. Amplified Bible
Words in parentheses () are my insertion.

ANOINTED Married Christian Men

    Because some women's lives may be at stake, succinctly stated, if we live in abusive, especially physically abusive relationships we need to seek professional assistance. If we've been hit once we'll probably be hit again. Until our husbands receive professional help our lives are in danger. Parenting classes also address some pertinent topics such as the proper communication of feelings. They may not be bad guys; in fact, they can be saved men. They can love their wives, but HIS problem can lead to her death. Women, please be careful, because it's when women in physically abusive relationships try to leave their domestic situation that most of them are more severely injured or killed.

    When we know for sure or have a really, really strong unction (spiritual sense-knowing) that our husbands are having sexual relationships with others, please take it seriously – life threateningly, because if our husbands were to contract HIV/AIDS our lives would be in danger. The same is true of husbands who believe their wives are having sex outside of the marriage. Men die, too. Amen. If our marriage vows have been broken in this manner, our spouse has broken covenant with us. We have to know with certainty we are not infected. If our spouse doesn't receive treatment or counseling to address the initial cause of the infidelity how can we be sure they won't engage in that life threatening behavior again? We can pray and believe God that our spouses sexual addiction to porn can be healed, or their overeating can be healed, but physical and sexual abuse of this type really demand we start to preserve our own lives along with the lives of our children (if there are any).

God hates divorce and separation but He loves HIS children. He sent His only Son to die for us and all heaven rejoices over one soul who repents. The day we repented of our sin we became His children, therefore, WE (YOU) are important to God. Individually, we each must realize we are important to "SELF". There aren't a lot of scriptures in the Bible on this topic because HIV/AIDS is a modern disease. There are, however, quite a few scriptures in the Hebrew Scriptures which address sexual misconduct within the family. The outcomes for the perpetrators in those scriptures are not good.

Women are not children, they deserve respect. Maleness does not give a husband the right or privilege to mistreat his wife or to behave badly, irrespective of the fact that he's the head of the house and head of his wife. Instead, he is held to a much higher standard of preserving, loving, cherishing, and honoring his wife. We have read these scriptures earlier in this work. When a husband loves his wife as Jesus does the church he will be willing to give, to sacrifice himself (his wants, desires, and expectations) for his wife. Jesus gave himself for the church.

Some men love to say women need to be

submissive to their husbands, but I'm confident that when husbands start loving their wives as Christ does the church there won't be as many issues surrounding wives being submissive. Being submissive does not mean being a victim of spousal abuse. Many couples think it's acceptable because they misunderstand the "submissive" teaching preached over the pulpit. Women who put up with this type of behavior allow themselves to be subjugated without speaking their thoughts in the marriage relationship. Oftentimes they are more susceptible to death from heart attacks than their contemporaries who communicate their thoughts and feelings.

  To communicate effectively what constitutes abuse the following pages contain lists, types, and instances from The Center for The Prevention of Domestic Violence. "According to the F.B.I. every 15 seconds a woman is battered in the United States by her husband or live-in-partner." (The Center for the Prevention of Domestic Violence) Remember the statistics listed at the beginning of this book states abuse happens every 9 seconds. So how many of the women in that 9 second time frame are abused Christian women being abused by their Christian husbands?   While there are no statistics available tracking the instances of men who are abused by their wives or live-in-partners, we can be assured that it happens more frequently than anyone knows. Physical, sexual, emotional, psychological, financial, and spiritual abuse are real. Those types of abuse that don't initially threaten our health can emotionally threaten our physical health; our lives. If we recognize ourselves, our spouses, our relationships within these pages, seeking professional assistance is necessary. Ideally, our spouse should attend counseling with us, but preserving our individual lives is the most important thing. Yes, we need to pray, but with our faith we need to move, make some decisions to devise some plans for survival.

Another sign that professional assistance might be needed is the absence of physical intimacy (sex) within the marriage. Men could have prostate issues which need to be treated by an Urologist. If he has diabetes, high blood pressure, or other physical ailments he may not be able to obtain or sustain an erection. He may be afraid to go to the doctor and feel embarrassed to discuss it with his wife. He may be angry and frustrated, also. He needs professional assistance.

As women we may experience dryness or pain during intercourse which can be treated by our Gynecologist. If we are pre, peri, or post-menopausal we may need to seek the assistance of our physician to deal with mood swings, cold sweats, insomnia, overheating, depression, etc. If we get extremely emotional, mean, or downright evil before, during, or after our period we may need to see our doctor, especially, if we find we are really tired during these times.

This is not a joke. Seeking assistance from medical and spiritual professionals is a sign of strength. It can be a source of strength as well. Sometimes, it's the last resort, especially for African Americans and other minority men. This has been the case historically. This doesn't have to be the case. Visiting these professionals can be a first step towards a blessed union and a long healthy marriage. This is important to consider since today most women enter the emergency room due to the physical abuse inflicted by a man with whom she's been intimate.

A second note of concern for women, especially, if our husbands rape us or uses the threat of violence it's important to admit this to ourselves first and then to a professional. If we have little girls in our homes we need to be watchful. Rape is not just a sexual act; it is a power issue. He may need to exert that power over our children. As a parent educator I know it is our responsibility to ensure the safety of our children making sure they are not being molested, raped, and/or fondled.

Today many women have children before they enter marriage. As we believe God for our mates we meet Godly men in church who we think are answers to our prayers. Many times they are, but please know many pedophiles seek women with children to marry so they can have ready access to their prey (our kids).

According to the American Academy of Child and Adolescent Psychiatry: 1. One in three girls are sexually abused and one in four boys experiences this pain. 2. Suicide was the third leading cause of death for 15 to 24 year olds, and the sixth leading cause of death for 5 to 14 year olds in 1998. What would have to happen to a 5 year old to cause that small child to want to commit suicide? I wonder how many of them were abused and too afraid to tell their mothers or some other adult. Many times the abuser will threaten to harm the child's mother, pet, or other family members if the child reveals what has happened in order to secure the child's silence.

As wise women there are some things we definitely should not do if we are living in abusive marriages: 1. Don't verbally threaten to leave. 2. Don't provoke our husbands. 3. Don't throw this book in his face literally or verbally by saying, "See I told you, you were wrong." 4. If we decide to leave, we should make a plan as secretly as we can, hide everything, then just go. If our lives are in imminent danger we should forget all this doing whatever we need to do to save ourselves.

As for abusive women who beat up on their husbands and kids, seek professional assistance. No one talks about the women who abuse, but there are many who do. If we are abusing our kids we might need Counseling, Anger Management, Parenting, and

ANOINTED Married Christian Men

Prayer. We can't continue to be the devil's pawn – we can save ourselves and our families. Men marry women and the woman becomes the mother to his children. These women can sexually abuse children, also. Women who are abusing their husband's children, stop it. Get help. Help is out there for women, too. We can live free from abuse or we can continue to commit these crimes (yes it's criminal) and we could end up living behind bars.

We have options: call 911, file a report, get a restraining order unless you know this will agitate him, get personal protection, in Ohio call the Rape Crisis Center Hotline at 216-619-6192, or the Domestic Violence Center at 216-391-HELP and nationally call 1-800-799-SAFE (7233).

Celia Wilson

My Beauty

My beauty does not come from what I wear,
Or what they say.
My beauty does not stem from make-up or jewels.
My beauty comes from things disregarded by fools.
It comes from my smile,
My gusto for life.
It comes from years of marriage,
As a faithful wife.
It comes from my ability to bring laughter,
Warmth, and charity.
My beauty comes from sensing other's hurt,
Or pain with sensitivity.
My beauty comes from who I AM.

ANOINTED Married Christian Men

THIS IS ABUSE

(The Center for the Prevention of Domestic Violence)

WHAT IS DOMESTIC VIOLENCE

DEFINITION: Domestic violence is the mistreatment of one family member by another. Most often perpetrators of abuse and battering are: a spouse, ex-spouse, boyfriend, ex-boyfriend, or lover. Most often victims of abuse are women and children. The abuse can be physical, sexual, spiritual, financial, emotional or psychological.

Celia Wilson

Types of Abuse

Physical Abuse
Pushed
Kicked
Raped
Dragged through the house
Poked
Held down
Slapped
Hair pulled
Restrained
Arm twisted
Squeezed
Tripped
Choked
Pinched
Thrown down stairs
Punched
Spitting
Grabbed
Threatened with a weapon
Suffocated
Threw objects at me
Locked in the house
Kidnapped
Bumped into
Burned
Banged my head in wall
Cut
Bent finger backwards
Pushed out of car

Sexual Abuse
Raped
Wouldn't allow birth control
Accused me of affairs
Told I was inadequate in bed
Said my body disgusted him
Accused me of sleeping with women
Friends wanted sex after abuse
Forced pregnancy
Distasteful sex acts forced on me
Beaten if I refused sex
Brought other women home
Criticized my appearance

ANOINTED Married Christian Men

Sexual Abuse

Told me I was fat and ugly
Bragged about infidelity
Made constant sexual demands
Didn't care about my pleasure
Withheld sex from me
Forced cohabitation

Financial Abuse

Took my money
Controlled the checkbook
All bills are in my name
Didn't know about assets
No money of my own
I had inadequate clothing
Sold my furniture
Had to account for every dime
Destroyed belongings I worked for
Quit his job
Never given enough money for bills
Forced to write bad checks
His wants came before family needs
Not allowed to go to school/work
Made to work
Spent money on drugs/alcohol
Forced to commit robberies
Forced to accept unwanted guilt gifts
Separate bank accounts/hidden

Celia Wilson

Not getting a better job/second job
Gambling
Not paying bills
Wasting money

VERBAL ABUSE
Yelled at
Called names
Nagged at
Called racial slurs
Put downs of women in general
Told no one else would want me
Always called stupid
Threatened to kill me
Threatened to hit/hurt me
Put down my family
Talked to as a child
Belittled important things I did
Put down my appearance
Constant phone calls
Told I was crazy/stupid/ugly/dumb
Told I was an alcoholic/drug user
Told the kids they didn't have to listen to me or respect me

EMOTIONAL ABUSE
Embarrassed me in front of others
Created crises so I had to pay attention to him
Living with his alcoholism/drug abuse

ANOINTED Married Christian Men

Constant demands on my time
Always had to agree with his opinion
Only allowed to see his friends, never mine
Had to do everything, even when sick
Always worried about his next step
Threats to hurt or kill me or the kids
Didn't talk to me – the silent treatment
Threats to hurt or kill himself
His suicide attempt
Couldn't have any privacy
Excluded me from my family members
Couldn't tell when he'd be nice or mad
Made me lie about how injuries occurred
Threatened to hurt family/friends
Threatened or actually hurt the pets
Not allowed to use the phone
Told me others didn't like me
Destroyed belongings important to me
Physically withdrew from me

SPIRITUAL ABUSE
Forcing you to practice his religion
Putting you down for your religious beliefs
Using religion practices to control you
Quoting religious script to justify abuse

Celia Wilson

PRAYER FOR YOU (III)

ANOINTED Married Christian Men

Heavenly Father, I love you so much. I love husband's name and if I am in an abusive relationship please show me, please give me wisdom according to Your Word in James which says, "If anyone lacks wisdom let him ask of God who gives to all men liberally and upbraideth not." You said "in the multitude of counselors, there is safety" so if my husband and I need counseling please open our hearts to seek and receive it. Help me to know if I can bring this subject up to husband's name without causing harm to come to myself. If I can't, Heavenly Father, I bind the spirit of abuse in this marriage. I bind the spirit of abuse influencing the abusive spouse. I loose that spirit from my house and from our lives in the Name of Jesus. I loose "the Spirit of Love, Joy, Peace, Patience, Gentleness, Goodness, Faith, Self-Control, and Meekness" to have freedom in our home, lives, and marriage. I bind them upon our hearts, Lord.

Lord, I pray for healing for husband's name from whatever happened or didn't happen in his life to cause such a deep hurt in him that makes him feel the need to have to hurt me. I pray the same for me if it is true of me, if I am abusive in any way. Father, if my children are at risk please show me in the Name of Jesus. Give me wisdom, Heavenly Father. Show me how to save my marriage and myself.

If husband's name has been unfaithful sexually please protect me from deadly diseases.

Celia Wilson

Your Word says, "Nothing shall by any means hurt me" and "Sickness and disease cannot dwell in my mortal body", because "By Jesus' stripes I am healed." I bind the spirit of fear that tells me not to go get tested, if I know <u>husband's name</u> has had sexual intercourse with others. Help me Heavenly Father.

    Heavenly Father, I know divorce and marital separation are not pleasing to You, but I know You sent Jesus to die for me, because You love me. I believe You don't want me to die in this marriage from being abused by an injured man. If this is my "way of escape", I pray You put Your protective hedge around me as I do Your Will. Your Word says, "No weapon formed against me shall prosper." The enemy would have me dead, my children injured, or living in fear, but I stand on Your Word which says, "I shall be saved and my whole house" and "As for me and my house we shall serve the Lord." This day You put before me life and death, I choose life, Father. "The enemy comes to steal, kill, and destroy, but You, Dear Jesus, come that I might have life and have life more abundantly." I receive the abundant life you have for me. I plead Your Blood, Jesus, over this situation, over our marriage, over <u>husband's name</u>, over our kids, and myself so our lives, peace, freedom, and love will not be stolen, killed, or destroyed in the Mighty Name of Jesus.

    Lord, I won't move until You tell me. I'll stay

ANOINTED Married Christian Men

before You to get a plan of performance if I am not in immediate danger. I'll "be still and know that You are God" so when I make a move "my steps are ordered by You" in the Mighty Name of Jesus. Father, I place our marriage in Your Hands to do with as You please. I renounce pride. "I decrease so You may increase" in our situation, but I need You to move now, Heavenly Father. Move now in my life in Jesus Name.

   Heavenly Father, if I am the abusive one in this marriage please forgive me and heal me. I give my spirit over to You the Great Physician, the Balm of Gilead. I plead Your Blood over myself and pray You put Your protective hedge around me and around my family so I no longer abuse and misuse in the Name of Jesus. Send me to the proper place for counseling, anger management, and parenting. I decrease today, Lord, so You can truly increase in my life. If I've hurt anyone please heal their wounds. I'm so sorry, please preserve, change, heal, and deliver my spirit, soul, and body in the Strong Name of Jesus.

Scripture references: James 1:5, Prov. 11:14, I Cor. 10:13, Gal. 15:22, I Peter 2:24, Is. 54:17, John 4:53, Deut. 30:15, John 10:10, Ps. 46:10, Ps. 37:23, John 30:30.

CHAPTER 6
THE SIGNIFICANCE AND POWER OF "WITHOUT SPOT OR BLEMISH"

ANOINTED Married Christian Men

    Hebrew history teaches us when animals were sacrificed on Jehovah God's altar they had to be free from spot or blemish to be acceptable to God. Similarly, Jesus had to come to earth in the form of a man to live a sinless life, in order that He might die, giving His life as a sacrifice without spot or blemish, for our sin. Remember, we learned that I Peter 1:18-19 informs us as follows, "But with the precious Blood of Christ, as of a lamb without blemish and without spot." And now we understand the precious Blood of Jesus will present husbands to wives as lambs without blemish or spot. However, first they must be presented to God as lambs without spot or blemish and Jesus accomplishes this for them.

    Now, how does this apply or relate to us as their wives? Remember, in

> Ephesians 5:22-29, **Wives**, **submit** to your own **husbands**, *as* to the **Lord**. For the **husband** is the **head** of the wife, *even as* **Christ is** the **head of** the **church**: and he (JESUS) **is** the **savior of the body** (of Christ). **Husbands love your wives**, **even as Christ also loved the church**, *and* **gave himself** for it. **That he** might **sanctify** and **cleanse** it

with the **washing of water by the word**. *That he* might **present** it **to himself a glorious church** (**wif**e), *not having spot, or wrinkle, or any such thing*; but that it (***she***) **should be holy and without blemish**. So ought **men** to **love their own bodies**, **he** that loveth **his wife** loveth himself. For no man ever yet hated his own flesh; but *nourisheth and cherisheth* it, **even as the Lord the church**.

Words in parentheses are my insertion.

Alright, I changed the fonts for emphasis. I hope it works. Let's examine this scripture carefully. The first thing we learn is vital. Wives are suppose to submit to their husbands AS TO **THE LORD.** <u>PLEASE NOTICE, the scripture doesn't say the wife has to submit to her husband if he treats her badly.</u> I don't know about you, but my Lord, Jesus Christ, never mistreats me nor does he ever abuse me. He never disrespects me. So in submitting to our husbands as to the Lord we are to expect our husbands to be "lord like". Amen. He isn't Jesus so I didn't capitalize lord, so he's not expected to be perfect as Jesus was. However, he is expected to be as much like Jesus as is humanly possible for a human man to be as he relates to his wife. If this wasn't important to the writer of Ephesians he just could have written, "Wives submit to your husbands."

Correspondingly, we learn the husband is the head of his wife. That coincides with everything we've always been taught in church right? Right! That's a good thing. Next, it says EVEN AS, what does that mean? It means the husband is the head of the wife just like – even as – Christ is the head of the church. What does that mean? The husband is not JUST the head of his wife to RULE and LORD over her, to order her around, or BULLY and BOSS her. No, he is the head of his wife just like, even as Christ is the head of the church. The husband is suppose to imitate, look like, and mimic Christ as the head of the church in his position as head of the wife. What does it mean to say Christ is the head of the church? In the books of Colossians and Ephesians, Paul

Celia Wilson

develops the concept of the church as the Body of Christ. Since the Church is the Body of Christ and Jesus Christ is the Head of the Body of Christ what does that mean? What does the head of a body do in relation to the body? The head - a healthy head - is supposed to plan and make the best decisions for the body. How many husbands are overweight from not eating properly or not exercising? How many husbands are in dead end jobs, under-employed, or unemployed from not making the best decisions to either obtain more education, or get a second or better job? How many husbands are drinking themselves to death, or drugging themselves into the graves, and not seeking help for their addictions? How many husbands are driving too fast, or living in the fast lane by having sex with others outside the marriage, whether they are women or men (for the men on the down low)? Many husbands don't love themselves. Tell me how they can love their wives? How can they take care of the body (their wives) when they as the head, can't focus or make good decisions for themselves?

  The eyes (eye lashes, eye brows), ears (ear wax, ear drum), nose (nose hair, mucus), mouth (teeth, tongue, and taste buds), chin, cheeks, jaws, hair, and scalp are all on the head. What are their purposes? With the eyes the head sees. The eyelashes protect the eyes. The eye brows give character to the face. The head needs to see so the body avoids danger, enters into healthy, safe, fun places. We can see what we're eating, where we're laying, and to whom we're talking. Seeing is very important. When a husband says to a wife, "I'm the head of this family, the head over you," is he leading the family in the best ways and places? Is he seeing the danger before hand and avoiding it for the sake of his wife? Is he providing for her so she lives in a beautiful setting? Does he groom himself well? Is he ensuring that she sees the good in his character by practicing gentlemanly qualities (opening her door, pulling out her chair, walking on the outside on the sidewalk, etc.)?

    With the ears the head hears what is important for the survival of the body. The ear wax and ear drums are for protection and the channel by which the ear hears and differentiates sounds. When a husband tells his wife he is in charge of her, she needs to be quiet and do as she's told (as if she were 5 years old), is he hearing all the threats to his wife and family? Is he hearing the sweet music of life that makes it a joy to be living? Is he able to differentiate between the garbage and garble in the world and the life giving voice of God? Is he able to really HEAR his wife? Does he really listen to her or even let her talk? Does he think she has anything to say worth his listening? Does he value the sound of her voice? Does he protect the sounds his wife and children hear?

Celia Wilson

The mouth (which houses the teeth and tongue) is used to keep the body alive, by giving it nourishment. The teeth ensure the nourishment is the proper size for consumption. The tongue makes sure only good nourishment is digested, or at least that it tastes good. It protects us from food that doesn't taste good. The mouth is where the bad food we eat comes out in the form of vomit. Without the mouth the body dies, unless one is ill and fed intravenously. Therefore, when a husband brags to his friends that HE'S the HEAD of his HOUSE, HIS wife, is he providing proper nourishment for her on all levels (intellectual, social, spiritual, physical, creative, and financial)? Is he protecting her from poisons? Is he making sure what she needs to consume in her life is good on all levels? Is he making sure what he provides for his wife is in the proper size? You know the right amount of water, starch, vegetables, fruit, protein, etc. Does she get the right amount of praise, verbal support, encouragement, compliments, and spiritual direction from her husband? Does he get rid of stuff that might make her or his children sick? You know what I mean cussing, yelling, fault finding, bossing, criticizing, ignoring (not speaking to her), and negative confessions? Does he pray for her and cover her in prayer? Does he speak God's Word over her? Does he conduct family meetings or read the Bible with his wife?

ANOINTED Married Christian Men

     The jaws, cheeks, and chin help give the face form, help to process food, and consume liquids. They help with the forming of words and hold the teeth together. Is the husband (who is the head of his wife) helping to give her proper form (the form of a godly, blessed, holy woman of God)? Is he helping her consume the proper nutrition in the form of solids and liquids literally food, but spiritual and emotional healthy nourishment, also? Isaiah 54:5, "For thy maker is thy husband, The Lord of hosts is his name…." Is he making her into the woman of God she is suppose to be by speaking the Word of God over her, into her, over, and into his family? He makes her by what he sows into her. Does he give her time to herself to pray, meditate, exercise, spend time with her friends, etc.? Does he run his hands over her body speaking health, beauty, and sexual satisfaction over her?

     Lastly, there is the hair and scalp. What are their purposes? Hair provides protection and is a fashionable feature. The scalp holds the hair and covers the cranium. So is the husband who wants everyone to hear and know his wife RESPECTS him (as he daily verbalizes he's the head of his house) providing protection for his wife on all levels? Is he in shape to do so? Is he physically agile? Does he have self-defense skills? Is he able to provide for her fashion needs? Is she well attired from head to toe? Do her undergarments match?

Celia Wilson

Are her teeth white: are they all there? Is he able to hold, comfort, and physically support his wife? Is he able and willing to provide her with the physical and emotional intimacy she needs? Does he cover her in word and deed? Are all her needs met?

    The head is the home of the brain, the thinking, deductive, reasoning, creative portion of the body. Is he providing all these things for his wife and family? If he isn't is he trying to find ways to improve his ability to provide these things for his wife? As the HEAD of the Body husbands have a great job to perform. Are they up to the task? I pray they are. The next part of Ephesians 5:23-29 informs us that the husband is the savior of the body. He has to be, because Jesus is the savior of the Body of Christ. How can a husband save his wife or provide a saving atmosphere when he is abusing her physically, emotionally, verbally, financially, or sexually? He can be her savior by providing all the things necessary to facilitate life for her; by pampering her, ensuring she is well cared for. Jesus came specifically to save the church. Do today's husbands come **specifically** to save their wives? Is that their purpose for living other than serving Jesus Christ?

    The scripture we read said, "Husbands, love your wives, even as Christ also loved the church." So the question would be how does Christ love the church? Jesus loved the church enough to die for her. Jesus loved the church so much that He gave up

ANOINTED Married Christian Men

all His heavenly power to come to earth to die for the church. Jesus loved the church so much that He He endured whipping and crucifixion for her. He sacrificed His "self" for her. How many Christian husbands do we know who live life this way in relation to their wives? Many of today's Christian men would have us believe the woman, the wife is the one who is suppose to provide the sacrifice of her "self" in marriage; that she's suppose to serve and obey. But didn't Jesus serve as He healed, delivered, and set people free? Yes. Where is the mutual serving in the family, in the home, in the marriage? Many men would say they serve by going to work, but many women also work, so this "service" has to be more than just going to work or running a business. It has to be an in home serving. I won't even go into how important a head would be without a body. If you sat a head up on a pedestal and just let it sit there what would happen to it? If there were no arms to feed it, neck to turn it, legs to make it mobile, etc. what would happen to that head? It would die wouldn't it? The wife as the body is vital to her husband. So, again, I say there has to be mutual serving.

  As Christ loved the church did he smack it, slap it, push it, stab it, or shoot it? NO. So how can Christian or so called Christian husbands say they love their wives when they abuse them? Jesus "gave himself for it." Are husbands giving themselves for their wives? Are they giving their time, their energy, their money, their prayer, their ALL for their wives? Until they do how can they call themselves the head of the wife? Until they start functioning, thinking, working as THE HEAD they are only figure heads, like the Styrofoam heads that hold wigs, or like the store that hires someone Black to act like they own it to draw the locals in when in reality it's owned by someone totally removed from the neighborhood. God made them the head, but their fronting. Their leadership is a bunch of empty filler. They may be the head of their wives in position by God's ordination, but they are not in purpose.

Why did Jesus love the church and give himself for it? He did this so the bible says, "That he might sanctify and cleanse it with the washing of water by the word." What does "sanctify" and "cleanse" mean in this verse? Maybe the answer is tied in to the word "cleanse" which means to make clean, clear. So, maybe Jesus loved the church and gave himself for it so the church would be set apart for Him only, and the only way to do that is by ensuring we are clean and clear from all evil and sin. The only way to do this was by dying for the church.

Well, our husbands don't have to literally die for us, because their blood would not save us. Jesus paid that price as only HE could, but our husbands can treat us as if we are so important by setting aside time only for us; by keeping all garbage from us and

ANOINTED Married Christian Men

our homes; by ensuring we are surrounded by the best in the best atmosphere. They can make sure we are clean physically, spiritually, and mentally by not bringing grief and heartache into our lives. Most of all they can speak the WORD of GOD over us, because the bible says, "with the washing of water by the word." Speak the WORD husbands: not your anger, your boyz ideas, or something you mimic just because a preacher said it. Speak the WORD of GOD to set your wife apart and to cleanse her from everything that's not like GOD. Praise GOD for husbands who do this, love doing it, and love their wives.

Why did Jesus do all this? That he might present it (the church, the BODY of CHRIST) to himself a glorious church. Wow, Jesus did all this because he wanted to present her to himself as glorious as he could. How glorious is a bruised wife? How glorious is a battered wife? How glorious is a cowering wife, a scared wife? I know she's not glorious. She's defeated, defiled, and debased by the man who is supposed to love her as Christ loves the Church.

The scripture goes on to read that the church (wife) is not to have spot, or wrinkle, or any such thing. Not one spot should be on her, not one blemish, or anything like it. It is Jesus' job to ensure she is without these things. Jesus lived and died to ensure the church remained free from these things.

Jesus wanted His church to be holy and without blemish. He didn't leave it to anyone else to ensure it was. How are modern husbands ensuring their wives are holy and without blemish in regards to how they relate to them? If they thought and believed their wives were holy how would they treat them, speak to them, relate to them, hold them, provide for them, and listen to them? How? It's a lot to think about isn't it? It's more than just viewing them as sex partners, cooks, maids, and slave girls.

      The Bible then says, "So ought men to love their own bodies." The men have to love their own bodies first, don't they? How many do? They are to love their own bodies the same way Jesus loves the church, after all aren't men part of the Body of Christ? It is then that they can love their wives properly. Believe me a wife knows if her husband loves or hates himself. The stupid vicious ignorant lie of the devil that says, "I love you so much. If I can't have you no one can. I will kill you rather than lose you." is just that - a lie. God is not in any of this, period. It is selfish, weak, controlling, manipulative speech directly spewed from the heart and mind of Satan. The Bible even says, "…he that loves his wife loves himself." So can't we surmise the opposite is true also, "he that hates his wife hates himself?" What are the signs he hates his wife? What are the signs he hates himself? Guess what, they are the same signs? We've already discussed them.

ANOINTED Married Christian Men

Jesus loves himself, His wholeness, His humanity, and sacrifice, but He loves and recognizes His position in the Godhead (the Trinity) and His Godness. Do husbands love all that makes them who they are: their humanity and the frailty that goes along with that? Maleness is not invulnerability. Do they recognize their place, their position is not in danger, is not threatened by their wives, because God ordained the man to be the head of the wife? It's a spiritual position no one can replace with a physically manifested presence. I don't think many do. Theirs is an awesome task.

      Paul seemed to think "no man ever yet hated his own flesh." I think and believe from the number of divorces, separations, abused, and misused women many husbands do not love themselves, their own flesh. Paul seemed to believe if the man loved his own flesh he would nourish and cherish it as Jesus does the church. WOW! It is my prayer that men, husbands everywhere love their flesh so they can love their wives as Christ loves the church.

      Ephesians 5:31:32, when speaking about the reason a man leaves his father and mother to cleave to his wife, making them one flesh says, "This <u>mystery is great</u>, but I am speaking with reference to <u>Christ and the church</u>." Then in verse 33, the writer tells each husband to love his own wife as he loves himself. Maybe that's what our men are doing, loving us as they love themselves. Consequently, since they have issues with themselves, they have to have issues with us. Since they don't or won't address their issues by either going to the doctor, the psychologist, the Christian counselor, the gym, for a walk, or taking their medication we suffer the consequences living tortured lives, in love, of course. PLEASE NOTICE, verse 33 says the wife is suppose to respect her husband AFTER he loves her as he loves himself and as he loves her as Christ does the church. It doesn't say she has to respect him if he hates himself. You can believe a wife knows if her husband loves or hates himself. It will be directly reflected in the way he treats her.

In I Corinthians 4:1, the writer invites us to consider that we are stewards of the mysteries of God. What is a steward in this verse? A steward is a house manager. Well, if a steward is a house manager, and the house manager is a steward of the mysteries of God, and the relationship between a husband who loves his wife and a wife who respects her loving husband can be explained and understood by the example of Christ and Church, then the husband should most definitely be managing his house within the mysteries of God.   Oh Beloved, this is why he is anointed. He can see within the mysteries of God. He can explain, teach, and work the mysteries of God. God anointed him to do this. The husband manages the house as his helpmeet guides the house. However, they rule together.

Yes, the wife should respect the GOD given position of husband just as David respected the GOD given position of King that Saul held. However, the first thing David did when he found out Saul wanted to kill him, was jealous of him, and didn't trust him was to run getting the heck away from him. He did not stay because that would have allowed Saul to hurt, imprison, or kill him. The enemy, male pride, and societal pressure has twisted and distorted the roles of husbands and wives, along with their relationship.

As I began to conclude this chapter I wanted to know how many scriptures in the bible spoke about the way a man should treat his wife; the way an anointed husband should treat his wife. Without going throughout the entire bible I came to this conclusion: A sane Christian man can't treat his wife badly without repenting and seeking help if he professes to believe in Christian tenets. He can't, it goes against everything Jesus is. Let's examine some scriptures regarding how Christians should treat each other juxtaposed with how Christian husbands should treat their wives.

Matthew 22:39, "And the second is like unto it, Thou shalt love thy neighbor as thyself."

Well, God wants us to love our neighbors, as we love ourselves. We already know men are to love their wives as they love themselves. It seems like the only prerequisite is you must love yourself. If you are expected to love your neighbor, would you consider the one laying next to you in your bed your neighbor, or is she closer? How much more should a husband love his wife?

I Cor. 10:23-24, "All things are lawful for me, but all things are not expedient: all things are lawful for me, but all things edify not. Let no man seek his own, but every man another's wealth."

So, just because a husband has the physical power to hurt his wife, doesn't mean he should. If we are not to seek our own wealth, but that of others, how much more should we seek the safety, security, and wellbeing of our spouses? He is suppose to edify her not tear her down.

Col. 1:10-13, "That ye might walk worthy of the Lord, unto all pleasing, being fruitful in every good work, and increasing in the knowledge of God; strengthened with all might, according to his glorious power, unto all patience and longsuffering with joyfulness. Giving thanks unto the Father, which hath made us meet to be partakers of the inheritance of the saints in light."

How can a spouse walk worthy of the Lord,

while abusing his/her mate? I don't think God sees spousal abuse as pleasing. If we are walking in patience, long suffering, and joyfulness do you think we're going to participate in spousal abuse of any kind? Do we believe the saints in light are abusive? If not how can one who is a partaker of their inheritance perpetuate such violence against another (his spouse) who is also a partaker of the inheritance of the saints in light?

Phil. 4:8-9, "Finally, brethren, whatsoever things are true, whatsoever things are honest, whatsoever things are just, whatsoever things are of good report; if there be any praise, think on these things. Those things, which ye have both learned and received, and heard, and seen in me, do and the God of peace shall be with you."

Thinking things such as: "You don't respect me." "It's your fault." "I'd be somebody if it wasn't for you." "I never should have married you." "Who are you talking to? I know you are cheating, Ho", are not in keeping with this scripture. Blame, mistrust, and all manner of thinking which negates God's Word should be avoided, unless we have actual proof of wrong doing. How can an anointed husband perpetrating spousal abuse honestly say I love Jesus, I'm a Christian?

Celia Wilson

Phil. 4:17, "Not because I desire a gift: but I desire fruit that may abound to your account.

Beating your spouse counts as what kind of fruit? Understand, because this book is about Christian husbands I focus on them, but these scriptures and questions pertain to abusive women/wives, as well. If our fruit is funky, nasty, or heinous what does our account in heaven resemble?

Phil. 2:1-8, *"If there be therefore any consolation in Christ, if any comfort of love, if any fellowship of the Spirit, if any bowels of mercies. Fulfill ye my joy, that ye be likeminded, having the same love, being of one accord, of one mind. Let nothing be done through strife or vainglory, but in lowliness of mind let each esteem others better than themselves. Look not every man on his own things, but every man also on the things of others. Let this mind be in you, which was also in Christ Jesus. Who, being in the form of God, thought it not robbery to be equal with God. But made himself of no reputation and took upon him the form of a servant and was made in the likeness of men: And being found in fashion as a man, he humbled himself and became obedient unto death, even the death of the cross."*

Since the husband is to assume the example of Christ in the marriage let's consider these words in relation to the husband. "Consolation in Christ",

ANOINTED Married Christian Men

"Comfort of Love", "Fellowship of the Spirit (Holy Spirit)", "Bowels of mercies". How can an abusive spouse say they exemplify Christ's qualities? Is beating a consolation in Christ? Is comfort of love treating an adult woman like a child or talking down and degradingly to her? Is the Holy Spirit fellowshipping with him as he tells her to shut up, or as he rapes her, or doesn't give her money to provide for her personal needs? Is he demonstrating bowels of mercies by isolating her from her family, by not allowing her to work, or go to school if she wants to, by cheating on her, or telling her she is stupid? Please tell me how being abusive is likeminded with Christ? How it proves as a husband he has the same love and is on one accord with whom Jesus has shown us He is? Are his rants, ravings, yelling, and constant reminders about how he's the head who's in charge being voiced in vain glory? When a King walks by everyone notices and responds accordingly. He doesn't shout to all the kingdom dwellers, "I'm the King. Look at me. Pay attention to me." His presence brings the respect and attention. His authority does this, not his mouth. Praise God.

     Is the writer saying Christians should have a lowly attitude esteeming and placing others above themselves? Wow, this has to also apply to Christian husbands, right? What about abusive Christian husbands? Should they take a lowly attitude esteeming their wives better than themselves? Wow, what if both the husband and wife were living with this Christ like attitude in their lives and marriage? How much beauty, meekness, giving, and forgiveness would emanate from their lives?

What kind of mind was in Christ? If the Christian husband has the mind of Christ, what does his wife's life look like? Oh, that's right, in order for him to have the mind of Christ he has to renew his mind with the WORD of God, not MAN'S OPINION, THE WORD OF GOD. What mind was in Christ? The scripture tells us, (My paraphrase) Jesus, being in the form of God thought it not robbery to be equal with God, but made himself of no reputation. He didn't focus on or make a big deal of the fact that He was equal with God. He didn't throw this fact into anyone's face. He didn't say for example, "I'm equal with God so you'll do what I say. You'll be quiet. I have authority over you and you'll act like it." Jesus took upon himself the form of a servant, Phil. 2:6-7.

This is awesome! Instead of Lording His "Godness" over mankind, Jesus came in the likeness or form of a man to serve humankind fulfilling God's plan to save humans. He restored the relationship God intended to have with us from the beginning. His service was to sacrifice himself for us. Wow, what a revelation. What if Christian husbands (who do have lordship over their wives and families) presented themselves as servants who serve (work, grow, learn, prepare: finances, homes, savings, and legacies) for their wives and families, instead of just verbalizing the words: "Woman, I'm the MAN of this house", "I'm in charge of you and this house, woman. Shut up and do what I say." Wouldn't his self-sacrificial service to his wife and family mean more, speak more loudly than any empty words he could speak? Wouldn't his wife and children honor, respect, and yes, even graciously submit to his lordship perpetuated by the authentic love and life MANIFESTED in the fullness of a loving MAN OF GOD? Oh, I believe they would. Let's look further.

Phil. 2:8-9a (My paraphrase) And being found in fashion, or appearance as a man, he humbled himself, and became obedient unto death, even the death of the cross. Wherefore God has highly exalted him..."

Look at these scriptures from other translations:

Jerusalem Bible: *Phil. 2:6-9a, " His state was divine, yet he did not cling to his equality with God but emptied himself to assume the condition of a slave, and became as men are; and being as all men are; he was humbler yet, even to accepting death, death on a cross. But God raised him high..."*

Living Bible: *Phil. 2:6-9a, " Who, though he was God,*

Celia Wilson

did not demand and cling to his right as God, but laid aside his might power and glory, taking the disguise of a slave and becoming like men. And he humbled himself even further, going so far as actually to die a criminal's death on a cross. Yet it was because of this that God raised him up to the heights of heaven..."

Amazing! What if we heard preachers preach this regarding how husband relate to their wives? What if Christian husbands tried to imagine what it's like to be a Christian wife; a wife dependent on a faith-filled man to protect and cover her in prayer while providing for her security? How would he then respond to her? If he wasn't doing these things his behavior might be unkind to hide or mask his failure. It might motivate him to submit even more to God in order to get a vision and a plan to provide for his wife and family, even to the point of working a second job, going back to school, starting a business, starting to save, just putting his wife first, or supporting her as she tries to reach some dream or goal. God would exalt this husband. God would bless this husband who is more humble to Him - who is obedient - utterly obedient to Him so that everything he touches, even his wife and children would be blessed.

I believe many men, because of America's societal history find it unthinkable to "become as a slave, to be humble, because in their eyes it's a relinquishing of power they feel they've never had in the first place. Maybe they believe if they relinquish their power to "God" now, not their wives, it would "De-Man-Ize" him in some way. "De-Man-Ize" means to take away some of his manhood. Look how closely this word is to "De-Mon-Ize. That's because Satan is the Father of Lies. He is the great deceiver who twists everything God does, creates, and says in order to create his own counterfeits so he can steal, kill, and destroy. In this instance Godly families and Christian men are hindered from attaining all God has prepared for them. Humbly serving his family would not make him less of a man; it would make him more of a Christ like man. Oh Beloved, how far Satan's lie is from the truth. What a terrible lie of Satan this is – a blinding lie that's devastating families and destroying men that we, society, and the world needs so desperately.

     If we read further into this chapter Paul tells us it's God working in the husbands who are submitted to Him as servants so they may be blameless and harmless, the sons of God. Their service occurs within their families to will and do of God's good pleasure without murmurings or disputing about or with their wives. If husbands are blameless and harmless, without spot or blemish won't their wives be also? I believe they will. I don't think this is a stretch of the Word of God, do you? Truly, this humbled man of God would shine as a light for his sons and daughters to see; for all to see.

Celia Wilson

Why? It's because this man would be holding forth the WORD OF LIFE. (my highlight from verse Phil. 2: 16a).

Women of God, this should be our daily prayer and belief for our husbands and for all men who would be husbands. Men of God this should be your prayer as husbands, and as men who are contemplating marriage. Marriage is about more than sex and the size or agility of the male organ. Marriage is about more than how many babies one can sire. Marriage is about more than men's sheer male muscles and certainly more than the loudness of their voices. Marriage is about more than the cost of our wedding dresses, rings, and the actual weddings. Marriage is about more than the number of guests at our weddings or the exotic locales we choose for our honeymoons. Marriage is a "spiritual union" in which husbands and wives submit to the Lord Jesus Christ, the Word of God, and the Holy Spirit. There's no room for ego, for "Look at ME, for "I". For marriages to succeed and grow in grace God must be the focus and Jesus the "eye" of our foci.

Someone said the "tone" of this book was angry from her viewpoint. Upon contemplation I somewhat acquiesce to her assessment. I am angry at the devil for blinding our eyes to the truth of the "Word of God". I am angry at the devil for the high divorce rate, even among Christian couples. I am angry at the devil for the high number of children growing up without fathers in the home. I am angry about the astronomical number of men locked up in prison, removed from society who need to be saved and home with their families. They could be there loving and serving their families. I am angry about the ever increasing rate of incarcerated women who feel lost. This "lostness" is due to their lack of spiritual covering by Christian men truly submitted to God. Therefore, they are turning to drugs, crime, and to the leadership of "lost" men. I don't apologize for the anger, for it has allowed the love and light of God to reveal His Word to my heart. It is with this love – His love – which was shed abroad to you from my heart that I wrote the words on these pages. I think my question to you is: Beloved, are you angry, too? Are you angry enough to begin to move in the Spirit of God to free God's people, empowering them to have healthy blessed families?

      It is my heartfelt prayer that the Body of Christ might mature. God's Anointed Husbands come forth in faith and power, in Jesus' strong and mighty name. Amen.

CHAPTER 7
WHAT'S SEX GOT TO DO WITH IT?

ANOINTED Married Christian Men

    There are two primary scriptures regarding the topic of this chapter. They are Hebrews 13:4 and I Cor. 7:32-35 which state: The bedroom is not defiled and married people care about the things of this world, how they will please their spouses. (Paraphrased)

    There are many things to discuss in this chapter: Extreme Sex, Sex Drives, Sex Toys and All Things Edible, Medical Problems, Infidelity, Newlyweds, Oral Sex, and others. So within the pages of this chapter we'll explore the above scriptures and others to address each of these areas as thoroughly as possible, as the Lord leads. I will tell it like it is, or ought to be, because that's the only way we'll become free in this area of our lives.

    Guess what a married "Christian" man is, a man. That's right they are men, and that means for the most part, if they are healthy they LOVE SEX. If we are participating in this sex with them, this means they LOVE having sex with us.

    Just in case some of us are wondering why I haven't said "making love", it's because I believe you either love someone or you don't. I don't believe we can MAKE love, but we can nurture the love we have for someone or the love someone has for us. We can also do things to cause the love someone has for us to deteriorate and vice versa. God is LOVE and His LOVE is shed abroad in our hearts, even when it comes to loving our spouses, after all without HIS

Celia Wilson

LOVE (Agape love); true eros (sexual) and phileo (brotherly) love will never be as fulfilling as they can be. Everyone may not adhere to this belief, but that is why the term "making love" will not be used in this book.

The Lies We Believe

The term "making love" has already been addressed. Human beings can't MAKE love, only God can. We hear the term all the time, so we just accept it into our vocabulary, just like the phrase "sleep with". We use "sleep with" to indicate that someone had sexual intercourse with someone else. We can all sleep together all day long. This wouldn't be a sin, except for the fact that it's slothful. However, no one would get pregnant or spread a sexual disease. "Sleep with" is actually to close ones eyes and enter into sleep with another person engaged in the same act. It has nothing to do with sex. Why do we use the phrase? It's because it colors, hides, or reduces the verbal impact of what we're about to actually do. I don't use the terms, either of them. I don't teach them to other people either. I believe in calling a frog a frog and calling a light a light.

Hiding is what the devil does, as well as operating in deception. How about the phrase "Lay down"? (Girl, he's trying to get me to lay down with him. I'm tired of lying down with him. Man, I'm gonna get that woman to lay down with me.) Another phrase used quite frequently is "going to bed with". We've heard it or maybe we've even said it. (Oh, I went to bed with him, or, He keeps trying to get me to go to bed with him.) Again, Saints, we could GO TO BED with each other all night long without one sin being committed. "Go to bed with", means two or more people lay in a bed. It doesn't mean they were naked. It doesn't mean they had sex. It doesn't mean they went to sleep. It doesn't mean they had sex and it doesn't mean any sin was committed.

      The sin occurs when sexual intercourse takes place. I wonder what would happen if we called it like it is. (Girl, that man wants me to commit adultery. I'm tired of sinning with him. Man, I'm gonna get that married woman to commit adultery with me. Man I'm gonna get that celibate Christian woman to commit fornication with me and immerse her immortal soul in turmoil.) See, that real communication is not sexy is it? Telling it like it is probably wouldn't draw the target in as easily would it? We have to wake up and stop being deceived by the words. If people approach us maybe asking them to spell out what it is they really want us to do would be prudent. We could turn around their "seduction" by spelling out what it is they're asking us to do. I bet adultery within Christian marriages would decrease. Maybe it wouldn't though. While, it's not sexy for a committed Christian to hear someone ask them to commit sin, thereby bringing judgment on both their souls, it might be enticing to Christians who have been taught that sex is something unspeakable or nasty. These Christian women might easily be enticed by a man who tells them exactly what he wants to do to them. Hopefully, once we addressed all these things in this chapter we won't be easily enticed by people outside of our marriages, period.

> Hebrews 13:4, Let marriage be held in honor- esteemed worthy, precious, (that is) of great price and especially dear – in all things. And thus let the marriage bed be (kept undishonored) udefiled; for God will judge and punish the unchaste (all guilty of sexual vice) and adultery. (Amplified)

Throughout, we will discuss aspects of sex and sexual activities as they relate to either honoring or dishonoring the marriage bed. We will define "vice" and "defile" so as to discern what "honors, is esteemed worthy, and precious of great price, and especially dear, as it relates to the marriage bed. We'll discern what this means practically applied to our lives as to avoid sexual vice and adultery. One might think just because a couple is married anything goes in the marriage bed, but if it is sexual vice or adulterous it dishonors the marriage bed.

The definition of "defile" is to make unclean or impure as (a.) to corrupt the purity or perfection of: DEBASE. (d.) to violate the sanctity of: DESECRATE. (e.) SULLY, DISHONOR. Can we agree adultery dishonors the marriage bed? However, once we move past adultery things tend to get muddled and confused. Some Christians think one thing is acceptable; others think one thing is a sin; others think another thing is nasty; while others believe all sexual biblical references pertain to everyone without regard for the historical context and subjectivity and objectivity of the scriptures.

Toys And All Things Edible

Sex toys in and of themselves are not wrong and are not vices. Edible panties and things of this nature, including oils, lotions, and creams are not dishonorable. The only problem would be if one of you were allergic to the solution and the other person insisted on its use. This act would be dishonoring to the other person, in turn it would dishonor the marriage bed. If one of you were afraid or apprehensive about using an item or device, the other has to honor that emotion in their spouse until the fear is worked through by realistic and honest discussions, reliable factual information or until the apprehension is gone. The Bible says "...**perfect love casts our fear.**" So discussing the basis of the fear is the only equitable thing to do. The spouse who's afraid would be dishonoring the other person in refusing to discuss the source of their fear.

Understand the issue may not be resolved in one night. Please don't argue, put down, or tease one another about the issue. Remember, many people have experienced abuse or had so much inadequate or incorrect information indoctrinated within them by parents and others that some people actually think "sex" in and of itself is nasty or is only useful for procreation. Sex for the sake of simply pleasure is seen as sinful. So we must be mindful that these types of mindsets and beliefs often impact some people's ability to interact freely sexually.

Some women have been taught that the use of items mentioned here are surely devices used only by whores, prostitutes, and loose women. So for a Christian man to even suggest to a woman who considers herself "holy" to engage in sexual activities involving these items is taken as a personal affront to her Christian character. For men who have been raised by prostitutes or women with questionable sexual lives often they resent the presentation of these items into their bedroom by their spouses because it brings up the painful images of their mother's immorality. These feelings are real and have to be addressed.

Again, many women (and some men) will wonder why any additional stuff is needed in the bedroom. They might think the spouse introducing the idea thinks they are insufficient or inadequate as a lover in some way. They must be assured that this is not the case. In doing so explaining that as their partner they want only to enhance what they already have or they think it would be fun to experiment. The items or devices aren't meant to replace or demean them because they are loved. This can be accomplished by explaining that as their partner we only want to enjoy and please them sexually. This aids our partners in understanding our motivation. This approach will alleviate one spouse feeling pressured in regards to toys and all things edible, because applying sexual pressure dishonors the marriage bed.

Sex Movies – Videos – DVD's and Sexual Addiction

Movies made of the two of you, by you are fine to be viewed by the two of you in your marriage bed. There is no dishonor or vice there. Vice is defined as: 1. (a.) moral depravity or corruption: WICKEDNESS. (B.) moral fault or failing. 2. Blemish, defect. Whatever the two of you deem as pleasurable in your bed is not "vice" and recording it for you to review at your leisure or pleasure is not "vice" either.

An issue would arise if you both died or

something traumatic happened to both of you simultaneously and someone else saw the movies. You both would be contributing to adultery, because someone else would be privy to the sexual intimacy of a married couple. This is a private matter. The discovery of the items might leave a "Blemish" on your marital image. Evil might be spoken of the good (the acts of pleasure you gave each other). Romans 14:16, "Let not then your good, be evil spoken of."

Also, in the Bible husbands are told to present their wives without spot or blemish, so husbands have to ensure that what their sex drives and imaginations cause them to create does not in any way blemish their wives reputations or their marriage beds. Similarly, we must not allow our use of pornography to cause us to misuse and demand satisfaction from our spouses, other people, or birth a cycle of constant masturbation to satiate our sexual appetite. This dishonors the couple and their marriage bed. Have no doubt that the movies made of our sexual exploits are pornographic. They're just our private personal pornography.

This could lead to the introduction of other pornographic material into the bedroom. Simply put, married couples watching (married or single) people engage in sexual intercourse dishonors the marriage bed and is a sexual sin or vice. Why? One or both of you will actually lust after these other people (because of our basic human lust). That lust will be satiated with each other. Plus, it's a form of voyeurism.

We should be turned on, sexually excited by our spouses. We shouldn't beat ourselves up if we "remember" things, events, or people from our past sexual episodes. That's one reason why God prefers us to WAIT until we're married before engaging in any sexual activity. Then this wouldn't be an issue. Most of us don't listen. Therefore, we have dirt to deal with. Often, this mental dirt isn't easily swept away. It will come back like an old photograph in our minds. With time, prayer, and fasting we can decrease the sexual impact of the image so when and if it "pops" up it doesn't trigger us sexually as it did when it was fresh. If we're conjuring up the thought there is another issue, because the Bible tells us to "cast down imaginations and every high thing (things that could become idolatrous) that exalts itself against the knowledge of God, bringing into captivity every thought to the obedience of Christ". (II Cor. 10:5) Words in parentheses are my insertion.

Sometimes outrageous thoughts creep into our minds. Also, Satan plants thoughts in our minds about other people we find attractive. It happens and it's going to happen as long as we're alive. We shouldn't add fuel to the fire, though. It's difficult enough to fight off the crap that seeps in, even when we are minding our own business, let alone adding more and more images for what, the fun of it?

Celia Wilson

The Internet has made this even more troubling, because access is much easier and allows us to access more content faster. This tool allows our spouses to be tempted by peep shows that include "T" and "A" nudity. This eventually leads to them being hooked, addicted, and captured by the sin of adultery without physically touching another living being. Mentally and physically they are spent. So either they have nothing left for us or they become sexual addicts expecting us to fulfill all their supercharged unregulated sexual desires at our physical expense. Really, it has been and still is devastating marriages: yes, even Christian marriages to this day.

What do we do if this foolishness has gotten the better of us? The Bible says in Proverbs 24:9a, "The devising of foolish is sin," such as planning to participate in pornographic activity (magazines, Internet, movies, DVD's, music videos, and some dance musical due to their erotic nature. Recently a television spokes person actually called Soap Opera sex scenes soft porn. What's that suppose to mean? It's only going to show enough sex to arouse you a little? See, that's another example of the lies we believe because of the words we're programmed to listen to in order to make sin more acceptable. Porn is porn, soft, hard, rare, medium, or whatever. If it leads to someone being sexually aroused, to masturbation, to the use of our spouses to relieve our sexual desire, or it leads to our committal of physical adultery it is sin. Let's look at steps we can take to empower ourselves against this vice:

    1.   Avoid looking at scenes of sex. Yes, even video games.
    2.   Only use a P.C. with the screen in the full view of your spouse.
    3.   Destroy all copies of anything pornographic in your home.
    4.   Avoid listening to sexually suggestive or sexually explicit songs (unless you and your spouse have planned a romantic session and you're setting the mood.
    5.   Don't dwell on, concentrate on, or intentionally think about past pornographic images.
    6.   If images pop into your mind, enter into an area where people are so you won't act on the impulse associated with the images.
    7.   If images pop into your mind, wait to have sex with your spouse once the memory and physical excitement of the images has long past. Don't let those images be your motivation for sex with your spouse.

8. If an image pops into your mind immediately begin verbally quoting scripture like: (**For Women:** *I Tim 6:6,* She that lives in pleasure is dead while she lives. **For Both:** *II Cor. 6:17,* Therefore, Come out from among them, and be separate, says the Lord. Do not touch what is unclean, and I will receive you. *James 4:7,* Therefore submit to God, resist the devil and he will flee from you. *II Peter 1:2-4,* Grace and peace be multiplied to you in the knowledge of God and of Jesus our Lord, as His divine power has given to us all things that pertain to life and godliness, through the knowledge of Him who called us by glory and virtue, by which have been given to us exceeding great and precious promises, that through these you may be partakers of the divine nature, having escaped the corruption that is in the world through lust. **For Men:** *Prov. 5:18-20* – Let your fountain be blessed, and rejoice with the wife of thy youth. As a loving deer and a graceful doe, let her breasts satisfy you at all times; and always be enraptured with her love.

9. If you become aroused by an image that pops up –RUN. I mean go for a walk or go to church to pray. Do

something constructive somewhere to keep your mind occupied. Go to school or volunteer somewhere. Remember the old saying, "An idol mind is the devil's workshop." Repeat these scriptures: *Phil. 2:5,* Let this mind be in you which was also in Christ Jesus. *I Cor. 2:16b,* But we have the mind of Christ.

10.   Pray and ask God to heal you of this addiction.

11.   Join a Spiritual Sexual Support Group.

12.   Seek Pastoral Guidance from a Spiritual Director.

13.   Purchase my study guide, *Overcoming in Life*.

14.   Learn/meditate on scriptures covering self-control, purity, the mind, imagination, adultery, victory, uncleanness, faith, healing, and deliverance.

If we rid our homes of these items we've begun to work on our growth. If an incident pops into our minds we should repent and move on. The less time spent dwelling on sinful thoughts lessens the frequency and impact. We can imagine our spouse as the object of our sexual desire increasing the pleasure we'll experience. Remember, having such items in the home presents a temptation to view them without our spouse leading to masturbation. This again is a dishonor to our mates because in our minds we are having sex with someone else using our bodies and minds to consummate the act. Remember, I Cor. 7:4, The wife does not have authority over her body, but the husband does. And likewise the husband does not have authority over his own body, but the wife does.

In the Amplified Bible we read: I Cor. 7:4-5ab, "For the wife does not have (exclusive) authority and control over her own body, but the husband {has his rights}; likewise also the husband does not have {exclusive} authority and control over his body, but the wife {has her rights}. Do not refuse and deprive and defraud each other (of your due marital rights), except perhaps by mutual consent for a time..." So while our spouses are obligated to have sex with us, we are obligated to ensure we don't abuse their bodies or our own.

Again, the habitual use of pornographic material can be a form of vice called "voyeurism" defined as: One obtaining sexual gratification from observing unsuspecting individuals who are partly undressed, naked, or engaged in sexual acts. One who <u>habitually</u> seeks sexual stimulation by visual means. Medical professionals are the best persons to diagnosis this disorder. While the actors, dancers, etc. are participating with the knowledge that someone else is or will be watching them, others in actuality should not be viewing them. This is what leads to the sexual excitement of the viewer, thus leading to the habitual seductiveness of this sin.

Adding Other People

Bringing other people into the marriage bed is adultery, period. This act is sin and definitely dishonors both partners and their marriage beds. It should be avoided. There are couples who do this. They love it and are happy and satisfied, but it could lead to jealousy, disease, fighting, divorce, and murder. It could lead to either one or both of them having sex separately with these other people. This is adultery, period. I guess the question is are they bi-sexual?

Oral Sex

Oral sex is not mentioned in the Bible one way or another. It is not mentioned as a sin. Some people refer to Romans 1:26-27.

> For this reason God gave them up to vile passions. For even their women exchanged the natural use for what is against nature. Likewise also the men, leaving the natural

use of the woman, burned in their lust for one another, men with men committing what is shameful, and receiving in themselves the penalty of their error which was due.

While, the writer was talking about lesbian and homosexual intercourse some people surmise that since a lesbian has no penis she must perform oral sex on her partner. Therefore, oral sex must be a sin and because she lacks the natural male sex organ she has exchanged the natural use of a woman. The same is said of men, except sodomy is added into the scenario. Men have mouths, tongues, and even fingers. We don't say it is the unnatural use of a woman when a man manually pleasures a woman. We call this foreplay. Isn't the same true of a husband using his mouth or tongue to pleasure his wife?

Some people believe oral sex is a natural part of a couple's sexual expression of their passion for each other. Problems arise though, if the husband doesn't satisfy his wife when using this method. She could (out of frustration and wonder) be tempted to sin with another man to try to achieve orgasm with this method. She could also be tempted to seek this form of pleasure from a lesbian, because she thinks a woman could bring her to orgasm. Of course either scenario would be a sin and dishonor the marriage bed because both are simply adulterous.

ANOINTED Married Christian Men

Some people don't like oral sex because they think it is nasty. The oral exchange of bodily fluids is too much for them. However, it can be utilized as a form of foreplay. It can be the entire sexual episode. However, having sexual intercourse, ejaculating, then performing oral sex can be and can seem distasteful to some. Many marriages end because of this. Many men, yes even Christian husbands, want to (I'd say even love to) engage in this form of sex. Conversely, many Christian wives don't. So the husband may eventually lose interest in sex with his wife. Then she feels inadequate and a void forms. If the husband forces his wife to participate in oral sex she then feels violated, cheap, and resentful, so again a void forms. Consequently, she could lose interest in having sex with her husband.

What should Christian couples do to avoid the "void"? They should talk about it. Indulge a little at a time if they both agree. Experiment a little. Husbands should not be forceful, but gentle and understanding. Wives should not be dogmatic and critical, but gentle and understanding. To just deny the other dishonors them both and the marriage bed.

If the wife performs the act the husband should in return spend time pleasing his way in the same way. Too often many husbands spend too little time on the wife's clitoris. When performed correctly this is very pleasurable for the wife. Sometimes husbands are too rough, too fast, or miss the organ (clitoris) during the process. They think just putting their mouths on her vagina rummaging around is suppose to please her.

Couples have to be patient with one another, communicate with each other, and practice without feeling like their being judged by each other. They are only trying to fully engage in the sexual experience with each other. During sexual intercourse both (BOTH) parties deserve to reach climax. It's selfish and dishonoring to avoid pleasing our partner. Be mindful of the fact that many marriages end because one of the spouses ventures outside of the marriage to find someone who will satisfy them in this manner, for this reason alone. It is senseless.

Remember, wedding vows state for better or for worse. If this is the worst thing we can experience in our marriages can we endure it to please our spouses? If this is the worst thing we'll experience in our marriages can husbands spend enough time on their wives to ensure she is sexually satisfied with this form of sex? Did we really mean those vows we spoke? Think about it, talk about it, and pray about it alone and together.

Then we must take into account our physical health. Open sores in our mouths, bleeding teeth and gums, cold sores (herpes) or some open, oozing sores on our or in our sex organs could cause health problems. We should avoid oral sex until these issues are resolved and our physician releases us. Also, I've heard of women being allergic to their husband's saliva, especially if he has oral health issues.

Anal Sex – Sodomy

As discussed in the last section people have historically determined sodomy to be a sin between men, because the men of Sodom wanted to rape the male visitors. The sin of Sodom was the disrespect of people's humanity, the violence perpetrated against others in the form of beating and raping (which is not about sex and expressing love but an exertion of power and control). The sin of Sodom was not sex or sodomy. The Bible says we should not seek to be free from slavery and those with epilepsy are demon possessed. We now know slavery is wrong, is evil, and definitely sinful. We now know epilepsy is a disorder which can be controlled with medicine or surgery. Sometimes those with the condition grow out of it. The Bible did not change, however, our understanding of these situations has, as should our understanding of homosexuals. As a result of humanity's outrage at slavery and the growth of our medical knowledge regarding epilepsy many people have been saved and live freely. The same thing should happen with Christendom's understanding of those not born heterosexual. Praise God.

Celia Wilson

    Some people know homosexuals are born homosexual and I guess blame God for these people being born this way. Do they view these people as cursed by God? Oh, maybe they see them as people needing healing; the medical and psychological communities don't. Other people think homosexuals choose to be homosexual and so choose to have this type of sex.

    Satan doesn't make people; he doesn't breathe the breath of life into them, God does. Therefore, those born lesbian, homosexual, bisexual, and intersexual (hermaphrodites) are born that way and the sex they have as a result of who they are born is not sinful. Those born intersexual really deserve our compassion because if surgery is not an option the lives they live can be torturous. How do they choose which organ is dominant, if any? How do they foster lasting intimate relationships? Ask them if they were born this way? The majority will tell you, yes. Forcing them to change or live "a lie" is torturous, even mean. Using scripture to perpetuate this is the same spiritual and verbal abuse used by men to justify treating their wives badly, plus it is bigoted. If they are not married because our laws won't allow it, it is not their fault. Allowing our laws to inflict prejudicial unjust pressure on them forces them to live in sin. God did not create them to be abused and mistreated, especially from those of us who are to imitate Him – LOVE. Many of them, especially the youth, commit suicide because we make it so hard for them to be themselves. This is horribly wrong and their deaths are senseless. They deserve to live and be happily married if they so choose.

Back to sodomy between heterosexual couples, although a discussion of sodomy would not have been complete without touching on all aspects of it. Sodomy is not discussed between a married (male and female) couple in the Bible. The men in Sodom were going to rape the angels of God, then Lot by sodomizing them, but none of that has anything to do with a married couple. If performed too vigorously it can be painful for both, especially the wife. Husbands should not force their wives to engage in this act. The decision to engage in this activity should be discussed and agreed upon by both parties. The matter won't be resolved overnight, especially if the wife is apprehensive in the first place.

There are some things couples can do to make this form of sex easier and more enjoyable. The use of lubricants eases entry. Having a mindset that this form of sex doesn't have to happen "right now" will allow time to practice anal entry a little bit at a time, until the wife gets acclimated to the feeling. At any point if she asks her husband to stop, he should honor her and the marriage bed by stopping immediately.

Husbands should spend time pleasing their

wives. Many husbands spend too little time preparing their wives by not paying attention to the other parts of her body. He has to spend time in foreplay, which is pleasurable for his wife, if he wants to engage in this form of sex. Sometimes, starting with a finger or two, then moving to entry of the penis a little at a time might feel better and be more comfortable for her. In order for this to not dishonor the marriage bed both spouses must be comfortable and agreeable.

If wives can't get into this husbands should not seek this one act from other women, even prostitutes. Bring the subject up every once in a while in a very romantic way. As wives we shouldn't just say no because not discussing it and being dogmatic dishonors the marriage bed. That is not to say we should forget that this orifice is used for other bodily functions. We should be mindful of the fact that anal tearing could occur, which is painful. I've heard of people becoming constipated and even women who are allergic to their husband's sperm during vaginal sex. What if she's allergic to his sperm during anal sex? As always, if we have questions we should speak to our physician.

We are always to put the well being of our spouse ahead of our own needs. There is no room for selfishness in the bedroom. Couples Phil. 2:3-4 reminds us that we should, "Let nothing be done through selfish ambition or conceit, but in lowliness of mind let each esteem others better than himself.

ANOINTED Married Christian Men

Let each of you look out not only for his own interests, but also for the interests of others." Placing our spouse's needs and interests before our own is paramount. It's the Christian thing to do. Having this mindset will stop both of us from putting pressure on the other. This will honor our marriage bed.

Pole Dancing and Stripping

Many Christians who have been raised traditionally or who have traditional values feel these acts are sleazy, because they are associated with strip clubs. However, in our homes with our husbands it can be very sexy. There are even classes to teach us the art of pole dancing.

Christian husbands find pole dancing and stripping very sexy and extremely erotic. If this is something men desire their women to perform it would be helpful if they remember their wives might be uncomfortable. Patience, kindness, tenderness, encouragement, and compliments will aid them in considering whether to engage in this form of entertainment. Women who've gained weight might be subconscious and not want to participate or expose and manipulate their bodies in this manner. Be patient. Encourage and compliment us on our appearance, our bodies, our looks, and our sexiness. Tell us how sexy we are all the time (not just when you want us to strip or pole dance). Touch us, kiss our bodies, caress our bodies so we'll know how much you love and desire us. Then maybe we'll have no problem dancing or stripping for you.

Husbands can dance and strip for their wives, also. We'll probably find you and your act sexy and stimulating. We can have fun with it and with each other. It's alright to laugh in the bedroom, in Jesus' Name.

Wives, remember, our husband's love us and want us. They desire us and find us sexy. Engaging in these acts is not degrading. However, since physical injuries are a real possibility to avoid doing things that could cause injury or that are really uncomfortable is smart. We can adapt the exercises to fit our abilities. Our husbands will love it.

Sex Drive

What if one of us desires or requires sex more often than the other? First, make sure there are no medical or psychological reasons fueling the zealous desires or causing the lack of desire. Depression impacts sex drives (it can cause some to hide internal feelings by focusing on physical sex or it can cause some to retreat inside themselves not being able to share themselves sexually). Past trauma impacts sex drives. For instance, some people who were raped or sexually abused become promiscuous, meaning they engage in sex randomly. If these people get married often times they commit adultery or desire sex quite often.

Sometimes though, it is just the opposite, they become frigid, bitter, harsh, and withdrawn. These people often end up as part of a couple. What must that be like for the spouse who loves and desires intimacy with them? Address these issues with professionals. Really, it's not Christ like to torture ourselves or our spouses. There is help and healing available. These issues can be discussed with Pastoral Care providers or Spiritual Directors, also.

If it's not one of these areas trying different positions or some of the topics mentioned in this chapter may enhance or increase our spouse's sex drive. That's right variety and excitement may cause our spouse (usually men) to desire more sex. Sometimes, for women too much variety, like the introduction or suggestion of some of the topics mentioned in this chapter can cause us to withdraw sexually. See, sex drives are chemical, but they are also psychological, spiritual, and physical. Diet can impact sex drives. Fatigue can impact sex drives. Medication can impact sex drives. It is vital that the couple investigates what's impacting the lack of, or powering the excessive sex drive if either one realizes the other is not being satisfied or feels they are being overly sexed. It is important that we verbalize if we feel we are in either situation.

Celia Wilson

Women, Nymphomania is a psychological issue played out physically. It is defined as, "excessive sexual desire by a female." If we are never satisfied, even when the sex is great, happens frequently enough, and orgasms are reached checking with a professional to ensure this is not our issue is prudent. Unchecked this can lead to adultery, disease, divorce, depression, and murder. It's important to recognize and address it.

Some women mistake the desire to reach orgasm for Nymphomania. They'll have multiple partners trying to find someone who can bring them to orgasm. This is not Nymphomania. If orgasms are lacking in our sex lives it is vital to tell our husband's what we need. Tell them where it feels good. Tell them where to touch, lick, or feel. Tell them how fast or slow to go. Tell them how much pressure to use. There are ointments and creams to use which make our vaginal areas more sensitive, thereby increasing our chances of reaching orgasm. If all that fails go to a professional therapist or physician.

If everything in the above areas are normal we can pray God make our sex drives more synchronized (where they meet somewhere in the middle). This honors both of us. One won't feel abused, used and tired. The other won't feel inadequate or feel like a sex fiend. Remember, the Bible says your desire shall be to your husband. Gen. 3:16c, "...yet your desire and craving shall be for your husband..." (Amplified Bible) It's the way God planned it. Enjoy each other.

Enhancements

Breast, butt, and penile implants are purchased quite frequently, but this should only be done if (YOU) really want them. If we do it for our spouses when we really don't want to we could become resentful and depressed. This could lead to divorce, maybe, even death.

Breast and butt enhancements can be purchased over the counter as temporary measures without causing long term medical problems, which is good. Penile implants are different in that this involves a medical procedure. There are exercises which can enhance our bodies naturally. If we are healthy this could be another option for many of us.

Then of course surgeons can implant enhancements for breasts and derrières, as well. Before any of these procedures are conducted, we should always meet with our private physician, as well as, the medical professional performing the operation. Remember, many people have died from complications during and following these procedures. Also, many procedures have gone drastically wrong. Some people end up permanently scared. Additionally, many of these procedures are really expensive.

We can try to be satisfied; pray to be satisfied

with our bodies as they are. A person who loves themselves is very sexy. They exude sensuality. The size of our sexual organs doesn't have to negatively impact our feelings of sensuality.

Husbands with smaller penis' can satisfy their wives by paying attention to their wife's clitoris and using their pelvic area to rub against this very sensitive area. They can also perform manual or oral sex, or use sex toys in combination with their other sexual techniques. It doesn't diminish a man's sexiness or sensual-ness to his spouse. It only enhances the wife's pleasure, consequently making husbands happy.

Men with an extra large penis must remember their wives are human. While women's vaginas can mold to fit a man, it's not a rubber band. Some women can only accommodate so much. All women's vaginas are not the same size. If we don't complain or don't suffer severe pain have fun. If we do be careful, be gentle. If necessary we may need to seek professional care.

Verbal Comparisons with Other People

Wow, this is a big NO, NO. This dishonors our spouse - their very existence - and should be avoided at all costs. We should avoid saying things like: "You can't kiss like so and so." "You can't do _____ like so and so." "_____ did _____ better than you." "I loved it when _____ did this to me." "Your breasts need to be larger like _____, see hers are really nice." "Why don't you start lifting weights like _____, I like the way he looks." "That's the way a woman should look, her shape is hot. I know what I'd do with her. You'll never turn me on like she does." These are just some examples I've heard of spouses saying to their mates. Surely, there are more verbal scenarios, but these get the message across. These are dishonoring statements. Repenting to God and apologizing to our mates is the right thing to do if we've ever made comments like this. We should also avoid statements like: "You don't know what you're doing in bed." and "You're a horrible lover."

     If we find ourselves attracted to certain attributes of other peoples human anatomy which our spouses lack there are ways to address them in this chapter which demonstrate love and respect for our spouses. Exercises like squats build the backside. Purchasing undergarments to enhance the butt, padded bras, dye, wigs, make-up, fake eye lashes and fingernails, and plastic surgery all address the issue. Consequently, we never have to use verbal comparisons with others to motivate our spouses to make changes in their appearance. We can let them know how we feel simply by saying something like, "Baby, I'd like to see you with a padded bra, I'd bet it be sexy on you." We could say, "Honey, can we start doing squats together just to keep ourselves in shape?"

Statements like these don't dishonor our spouses. They don't tear down or hurt our spouse's feelings or spirit. That old saying, "Sticks and stones will break your bones, but words will never hurt you." is a lie from the pit of hell, because words are spirit. They either minister life to someone or destroy and damage someone's spirit. John 6:63b says, "The words that I speak to you are spirit, and they are life." It's our choice to either speak words promoting life in our spouses or words that cause harm. Either way we need to understand that the words are alive. If we approach this desire to enhance our spouse's physical attributes from the standpoint of: "I love you, you are enough for me" our spouses might be more receptive to hearing our views. They may not agree to undergo major procedures, or purchase certain items or even join an exercise class, but at the end of the conversation we haven't damaged their spirit. Isn't that the most important thing?

Since we love our mate's physical attributes we should tell them by all means, all the time. Praise works. Praise can motivate our mates to make or keep up with physical improvements and healthy choices more than any comparisons with others.

ANOINTED Married Christian Men

Dishonoring speech dishonors the spouse, the marriage, and the marriage bed. **Remember, our speech should minister "grace" to our mates.**

From Dreams – To Reality

As they sip at their wine
Together they just dined
And he tells her that she's so fine, so fine.

With the music turned down low
In her ear he whispers soft and slow
While their minds glide together in a rhythmic flow.

As they lay down on the floor
With the wind knocking at the door
Wishing they could stay here, forevermore.

When he kisses at her cheek
She begins to feel so weak
Knowing it won't be long before they reach that splendid peak.

As he kisses on her lips
And runs his hands o'er her hip
She thinks at this point, her heart beat will skip.

But as their bodies entwine
It gets to be so divine

Celia Wilson

They end up in a wonderful love design.

As their yearnings are filled
Only God could have willed
That the feelings inside them be so deeply instilled.

When the sun started to beam
He awoke from his dream
And began to remember how real it all had seemed.

A quick glance to his side
Made his whole world open wide
Because the feelings that engrossed him,
He could not possibly hide.

Now, his mind's all in a wonder
And his heart beats like the thunder
As his eyes gaze at the slender figure
Lying underneath the cover.
He realizes at last,
That he had finally grown to love her.

Music

Many Christians feel it is a sin to introduce "secular" (that is non-Christian) music into their holy homes and bedrooms. It's up to each couple to decide. Music in and of itself is not sinful. The lyrics, what you're doing, and with whom you're doing it with matters, not whether the songs or music are created or produced by Christians. There are Christians who sing secular love songs. Does this make their songs sinful? There's nothing wrong with setting the mood for romance with music, candles, fragrance, lighting, and food. If one spouse really needs or wants to listen to music during sex when the other doesn't, that can be an issue. Although, Luther, Smokey, Barry, Teddy, Baby Face, Joe, Earth, Wind and Fire, etc., have been known to steam up many a bedroom. Sexy music and sensual conversation can act as real aphrodisiacs.

Some prefer Jazz or Christian instrumental music as alternatives to secular music. It's not a sin to engage in sexual intercourse while listening to Christian music or Christian instrumental music. God loves us to enjoy sex, that's why He made us the way we are. The Bible provides us with romantic renderings in Song of Songs, wherein we find the very sensually romantic encounters of loving married people.

It's not wise for dating or engaged (celibate) couples to listen to secular music, though. It can and often does lead to fornication. **Remember, words are spirit and they are powerful.** Listening to words about physical intimacy, love, and sex can stimulate some of us to the point that we chose to give in fulfilling the ignited desires between us.

Celia Wilson

Playing

Role play, dress up in costumes, chase each other around, tickle each other, and go out on dates. Have fun enjoying each other.

Extreme Sex

For those who are into S&M, bondage, domination, or cross dressing if your spouse isn't into the same thing there will be problems. The discussion surrounding these issues would have spared both of you had it taken place before your marriage. This is not the type of conversation to bring up in the middle of the Honeymoon or after a child or two. Doing that would mean the topic was a hidden issue. Hiding things is no way to enter into marriage, especially around sex, which is an extremely spiritual part of a couple's connection.

If one spouse is not into the others needed extremes it would behoove the one who is to seek professional counseling so as not to seek this "extreme sex" from outside sources. Seeking satisfaction outside of the marriage would dishonor the marriage, their spouse, and their marriage bed. It might help to understand why one needs extremes in their sex life. If abuse is the source, or some sort of physical defect, or something psychological it

Medical Problems

We broached this topic earlier in this book, but it bears delving into more deeply. It deserves dedicated attention. High Blood Pressure, Diabetes, Obesity, Heart Disease, Arthritis, Enlarged Prostate, Prostate Cancer, Fibroids, and other medical conditions can seriously impair couples sexual desires and sex lives. For many people a sexless marriage is not necessary. God does not desire his children to live sexless lives. That's why some priests fell into sin. Seeking medical advice from one's private physician should not be avoided. Those without insurance can go to a free clinic, while veterans can avail themselves of local VA Hospitals. Couples can confront these medical issues before they're impacted negatively. This is very important.

The impaired spouse can still please the other if it won't cause them physical harm. By utilizing some of the techniques mentioned earlier their spouse can experience all the joys of sex. Why should the healthy spouse suffer because of their mate's sexual impairment?

It might be difficult to admit there is something wrong, but using age or some other excuse is no excuse. It might be difficult to admit pride is prohibiting us from acknowledging and continuing to ignore our spouse's sexual needs. Why? Because our ability to perform according to some perceived standard is limited. This is selfish. Address the issue. As a couple speak to a Psychologist, Christian Counselor, or Pastoral Care Provider in case there are dormant issues on a psychological (emotional) or spiritual level impeding the impaired spouse from agreeing to satisfy their spouse. Do this after the medical professional has given advice or treatment regarding any physical problems.

There are also medications that can hinder, impair, or enhance one's sex drives. These should always be prescribed and monitored by a professional physician. We should always consult our physician.

The Word Wins

When old habits come to haunt you
Use the Word that Jesus taught you.
Keep your mind and watch your thoughts
Because that's where the battles are fought.
Listen for God's still small voice.
Just obey Him and rejoice.

ANOINTED Married Christian Men

Masturbation

It has been the author's experience that predominately Caucasian church leaders teach singles masturbation is acceptable, while predominately African-American church leaders teach masturbation is wrong. Therefore, married African–American Christians usually believe masturbation is a sin, while Caucasian Christians tend to believe it is not a sin. There's one thing to note regarding some people who won't masturbate because they believe it is a sin. Some of these Christians will fornicate as an acceptable alternative knowing IT IS a sin. As Christians we tend to lean toward scripture to teach masturbation is sinful instead of the medical community. The medical community purports masturbation is a normal human function.

In actuality the Bible's depiction of masturbation is quite different than we've been taught. Purification laws were instituted during biblical times to ensure those offering sacrifices to God were clean. I purport that they also ensured the health and safety of the populace. They did not have antiseptics, sterile packaged bandages, lovely hot water washing machines, detergents with bleach additives, or bathrooms with faucets. Therefore, when we read all the stipulations and rules regarding bodily secretions in Leviticus it was not because the people were sinful. They were to promote the health and safety of the people and Jesus took care of our need to offer sacrifices to God. We are now clean because of His sacrifice.

There were so many detailed laws that no one could live up to the strictness with which they were applied. Therefore, Jesus, in His coming fulfilled all the Law: Matt.5:17, "Do not think that I came to destroy the Law or the Prophets." Romans 10:4, "I did not come to destroy but to fulfill. For Christ is the end of the law for righteousness to everyone who believes." Galatians 3:23-25, "But before faith came, we were kept under guard by the law, kept for the faith which would afterward be revealed. Therefore the law was our tutor to bring us to Christ, that we might be justified by faith. But after faith has come, we are no longer under a tutor."

Leviticus 15:2-7 is a discussion between Moses and Aaron, in which the elder prophet tells Aaron any man with a discharge of pus, blood, mucous, and semen is unclean until evening, meaning he's not to be touched by others. Anything he or his discharge touched would be considered unclean. All had to be washed and cleaned. All remained unclean until evening. This information found within the Levitical Laws provided guidelines to follow if certain conditions presented themselves. The actual male discharge is not called a sin, but the condition of having the discharge remain on people and items caused an unclean situation and unclean people. Throughout scripture being unclean is considered a sin.

Similarly, Leviticus 15:16-18, 32 discusses when the emission of male semen presents an unclean situation. The emission could be nocturnal emissions (wet dreams) occurring while men sleep. Why would God consider something which happens unconsciously a sin, something which the person has no control over? He doesn't. The scriptures again tell Israel what to do in case the situation arises.

There is no mention of women's sexual discharges. Why it's not addressed specifically will not be examined in this venue. Although, one could surmise what goes for men applies to women, also. If we consider female sexual discharge as we do their menstrual discharge in regards to Leviticus we must admit those women who were considered unclean were removed from the city. We don't do that today. Why? Sanitary napkins, tampons, feminine wash, even perfumed versions of these items are available addressing the unsanitary conditions menstruation caused historically. The same is true of women's sexual discharge: sheets, clothing, etc., can all be washed removing anything unsanitary.

Suffice it to say if masturbation is used to curb, quench sexual desire which could lead to adultery it is not a sin for husbands and or wives. If it is used habitually and one's spouse is not removed

Celia Wilson

from the relationship for an extended period of time, there may be underlying issues to address. What if we don't know what the issue is? Wouldn't it behoove us to pray or seek professional counsel to find out what it is? It's an issue because consistent self-sexual gratification can delete/deplete, as it were, our ability to perform effectively sexually for and with our mates.

There is a scripture which can be applied to men and women regarding this issue, although it doesn't mention the word masturbation per se. Psalm 4:4, "Stand in awe and sin not: commune with your own heart upon your bed, and be still. Selah." If we believe masturbation is a sin or if it has become habitual this scripture can be prayed to satiate ones desire. Being still on your bed can be understood as not moving to masturbate. Communing with your own heart on your bed can be understood that you are to pray, meditate in bed instead of masturbating. So let me Celianize this: God is awesome! You believe this right? Don't sin. He's able to calm your loins. Pray and meditate in the spirit in bed. Don't masturbate, be still. Realistically, for some cessation will happen quickly, but for others this will be a challenge.

ANOINTED Married Christian Men

Be Still

Be still and know that I Am God
Is the plea the Father sends
To have you rest inside His love
And stop following worldly trends.

You don't have to help God out
Or boost Him on His way
For all the promises He's made
Will, in time, surely come your way.

Be still and know that He is God
And stop running your own life
Let God work His perfect Will
And let him make you a wife.

Sex as a Weapon

Eph. 4:26, "Be angry, and do not sin. Do not let the sun go down on your wrath."

Couples should never use sex as a weapon to punish or get back at one another. Sex is not one of the weapons of our warfare, Amen. Using it as such is a form of passive aggression. If there is another issue going on talk about it, resolve it, or agree to table it until later. We have the power to keep our sex lives free of "stuff". The Bible admonishes couples not to deny their spouses sex unless they both agree to refrain for a time to pray and fast.

Some men use hard, almost punishing sex to "teach their wives a lesson" about who's boss, but this is not right either. Often it borders on rape and not only is it a sin, it's a crime. Purposefully hurting a man's penis in any way is never right either. Teasing each other verbally or with visual enticements then not allowing our spouses to partake of our sexual pleasures is also dishonoring.

Being angry is not a valid reason to deny our spouses sex. Actually, having sex might help us communicate what made us angry in the first place. Sexual disconnecting for any reason other than illness, fasting, praying, or separation dishonors the marriage, the spouses, and the marriage bed.

I Corinthians 7:32-35

In the beginning of this chapter two scriptures were mentioned which undergird this section of this book? I Cor. 7:32-35 is one of those scriptures and reads as follows:

> *My desire is to have you free from all anxiety and distressing care...But the married man is anxious about worldly matters, how he may please his wife. And he is drawn in diverging directions- his*

> *matters are divided, and he is distracted {from his devotion to God}..., but the married woman has her cares {centered} in earthly affairs, how she may please her husband. Now I say this for your own welfare and profit, not to put {a halter of} restraint upon you, but to promote what is seemly and good order and to secure your undistracted and undivided devotion to the Lord. (Amplified)*

    It would be nice to have a satisfying sex life free from anxiety and distressing care, but as long as we're married this will not be our reality, because we are bound to care about what and how to please our spouses. As wives we need to understand husbands have many things vying for their attention; most of them being centered upon pleasing and taking care of us. Celebrating, rewarding, and honoring our men with as much sex as they want would surely keep them focused strengthening their resolve to be the best husbands and lovers they can be. If we think of sex as a marital ministry our husbands and pleasing them will be a central focus of our marriages.

    Husbands the same is true of how you approach us. We need you to do more than just WORK for us. Work at telling us lovingly, sensually, and demonstratively how much you love us by satisfying our sexual desires and ministering to us as if we're the finest sexiest women in the world. The Bible said this will profit you and be to your welfare. It will promote good order in the bedroom or wherever we choose to minister to one another. This type of blessed marital sexual activity will promote and lead to an undistracted and undivided devotion to the Lord, because sexual vice, adultery, divorce, depression (centered around sex), dismay, and dissatisfaction will not be an issue in our marriages.

Forbidden Sin

Alas, I wear another's ring,
But he doesn't see my hopes and dreams.
The thoughts of you come into mind,
Your smile so sweet, your words so kind.

When you look at me – you pierce my soul.
You seem to sense I've lost control.
Our glances are so strong as we pass,
Others notice our eyes are longing for romance.

You fine, intelligent, strong beautiful man.
I've already given another my hand.
To fulfill the fantasies I hold toward you,
Would cause my world to come unglue.

My Lord has spoken – adultery is wrong,
But my body burns as I listen to love songs.

ANOINTED Married Christian Men

I pray the desire to hold you ceases.
To feel your manhood inside me,
the desire decreases.

The thoughts surpass just physical pleasure,
But encompasses conversation and laughter.
To sit together and read a good novel,
To share our goals, experiences, travel.

Life's too short you can't die in sin,
From having affairs with married women.
I'd not put you through such a test,
To have our lives end up in a mess.

This forbidden sin I lately contemplate,
Would surely seal, condemn my fate.
Alas, my love, I must remain true,
To God above and my husband, too.

Infidelity

I addressed this issue in the book earlier, but it has a lot to do with our desire to engage in sexual activity with each other. The spouse who was unfaithful was just that "UNFAITHFUL". This unfaithfulness was not just regarding sex, it goes deeper than that. The act was a physical and spiritual infidelity. For the faithful spouse this was devastating to their "Personhood = Manhood or Womanhood." Consequently, it must be understood that their ability to trust the unfaithful spouse in all areas, including sexually has been damaged, if not destroyed.

If the unfaithful spouse lied about the affair, maybe they were lying about loving and wanting their mate, finding them desirable, going to the grocery store, going to get their hair done, or to wash the car. Thoughts like these may be going through the faithful spouse's mind. They don't want to be hurt again, even if they've forgiven the spouse who was unfaithful. The dynamics will differ if both partners were unfaithful, because either they will both forgive each other or the distrust will grow, poisoning their marriage even more. This does happen.

Blame is not to be placed on either spouse. Infidelity is just the symptom of a deeper relational problem. They need professional spiritual help to delve into this spiritual illness. Was a sexually transmitted disease brought into the marriage? If not, how can the faithful spouse trust they won't contract the disease in the future? Where is their peace to be found? Surely, peace can be found in their faith, but this could take some time. Was a child conceived during this tryst? If so this will make a whole other heap of problems with which they have to deal? I'm not trying to make anyone feel bad or make a situation worse. I'm trying to help couples understand all the thoughts that might hinder faithful spouses from moving forward once they've been so deceived. It's important, vitally IMPORTANT to understand the damage caused when we're unfaithful.

Then there are the emotional issues: hate, regret, sorrow, revenge (don't do it), unforgiveness, self-loathing, loathing the unfaithful spouse, anger, self-blame, distrust, etc. There are probably many more emotions not mentioned here. These must be addressed and healed one by one, in order to heal the relationship and sex life.

What would happen if the unfaithful spouse tried to introduce something new sexually into the relationship? Would the wounded spouse think the technique was something done with the adulterous other party, spurring them to cringe inside at the thought of doing something new with their unfaithful mate? To be honest they may not want to have sex with their unfaithful partner at all. It will take a lot of patience and much prayer. The unfaithful partner has to do this without being angry towards them as they navigate their way through this. Feeling angry at oneself for engaging in an adulterous relationship is normal. Hopefully, managing these feelings will be helpful in leading to healthy ways of dealing with the breach in the marriage.

Be encouraged, don't give up because many

Celia Wilson

Christian couples have come back from these marital issues and are now thriving. How'd they do it? "Perfect love casts our fear." is what I John 4:18b says. This is mature love that understands all people make mistakes, even our spouses. In the Amplified Bible the LOVE chapter we read:

> I Cor. 12:4-8, Love endures long and is patient and kind; love never is envious nor boils over with jealously; is not boastful or vainglorious, does not display itself haughtily. It is not conceited – arrogant and inflated with pride; it is not rude (unmannerly), and does not act unbecomingly. Love {God's love in us} does not insist on its own rights or its own way, for it is not self-seeking; it is not touchy or fretful or resentful; it takes no account of the evil done to it – pays no attention to a suffered wrong. It does not rejoice at injustice and unrighteousness, but rejoices when right and truth prevail. Love bears up under anything and everything that comes, is ever ready to believe the best of every person, its hopes are fadeless under all circumstances and it endures

everything {without weakening}. Love never fails – never fades out or becomes obsolete or comes to an end.

In the relationships that have survived adultery those couples may have utilized these methods, also.

Forgiveness – Godly forgiveness, which understands people can't earn or deserve our forgiveness

Humbleness – Void of pride and entitlement

Self-Sacrificial Love

Unselfishness

Time - Remember the old adage "Time heals all wounds" or is it "Time heals old wounds"?

Talking – Intimate, deep, truthful, real talk.

    If it seems impossible to transverse these negative marital waters seek the help of Spiritual Guidance Providers or other professional counselors. This is a course of action that couples should investigate, anyway. Some couples don't survive infidelity. If yours does, thank God and praise Him daily for what you have. I'm sorry I don't have any "sure" answers for couples faced with this dilemma.

Celia Wilson

All people, all couples, all marriages are different and the outcomes they experience will differ, also.

One thing taking place in some homes is the couple continues to stay in the same house for the sake of the children or due to financial concerns. Notice I didn't say live together or remain married. These people aren't LIVING they're existing. They aren't married, because even the word MARRIED suggests intimacy, committed-ness, sanctity, and ministry. They stay in the same house void of ANY intimacy, especially sexual intimacy which can be a torturous existence. This is dishonoring to both partners. Choose either to begin to repair the relationship or release each other.

Some people believe infidelity is the one exception to the (Don't Divorce) directive in the Bible (Matt. 19:7-9), regardless of whether clergy says the marriage has to be saved. It actually says Moses allowed divorce in the case of fornication. A married woman can not commit fornication because sex after marriage with someone other than her husband is called adultery. However, Jewish customs did allowed a husband to divorce his wife if he discovered she had committed fornication and was not a virgin on their honeymoon.

To help faithful spouses not think more highly of themselves than they ought to think the following scripture might help them think soberly and remain grounded. (Romans 12:3d, e)

ANOINTED Married Christian Men

> Matt. 5:27-28, 32a, You've heard it said to those of old. You shall not commit adultery. But I say to you that whoever looks at a woman to lust for her has already committed adultery with her in his heart. But I say to you that whoever divorces his wife for any reason except immorality causes her to commit adultery.

The same can be said of a woman lusting after a man. If we've ever thought about it, it's just as much of a sin as if we'd done the deed. Therefore, there's no room for our feeling all self-righteous like we're better than our spouse. Amen. This also answers the question posed above – adultery is immoral, hence divorce is permitted. Where does that leave those suffering through adultery? It goes back to the chapter on abuse. God doesn't want us to live tortured lives or live our lives in peril of death due to the actions of unfaithful unscrupulous spouses. Both partners deserve to LOVE and live holistically, with a spouse they can LOVE in return or they can live alone being safe and content. Amen.

Gay/Lesbian Spouses and Men on the Down Low

Celia Wilson

This topic is vitally important because many Christians and non-Christian wives are dying due to their acquisition of HIV/AIDS. HIV/AIDS is not the only possible sexually transmitted disease these couples are liable to encounter – Hepatitis and Herpes are just some of the others. Consequently, many babies are born only to die from the disease having been passed to them by their mothers. It's a horrible, sad, senseless situation. These wives are being infected by husbands (yes, even Christian husbands) who are secretly gay, living on the "Down Low". Living on the "Down Low" occurs when men lead seemingly heterosexual lives with their wives while secretly sexing either their committed homosexual partner or their indiscriminate sexual partners.

Our Christian attitudes and beliefs about homosexuality are directly impacting or driving this atrocious situation. Space does not allow a full investigation or this subject in this venue. Suffice it to say, lesbians and gay males in heterosexual marriages who are having sex with those of the same gender place their spouses in a truly unfair and dangerous situation.

Those who find themselves within the lines of these pages must find a way to make life safer for themselves, their spouses, and their children. Some homosexual spouses leave the marriage after telling their mates the truth about their sexuality, while some leave without disclosing the truth. Some try to remain in the marriage without telling their spouse the truth until they find out they've contracted a disease. Telling a spouse about your homosexuality while telling them you may have infected them with a potentially fatal sexually transmitted disease is cruel. Still others tell their spouses the truth and together decide how to move forward, ensuring the health and safety of all those involved.

The unsuspecting spouse deserves to know. They deserve to live healthy lives. Those who are lesbian or gay deserve to live freely, without guilt, fear, and hiding. The truth will honor both of them. There are professionals available to help with these discussions.

Away From Me

When you're gone away from me
It's hard to understand,
Why a girl so much in love
Must be separated from her man.

When you're gone away from me
I sit and wonder why,
But wondering when you're not here
Only makes me cry.

When you're gone away from me

Celia Wilson

They say our love increases,
But you don't have to be away
For my love never ceases.

When you're gone away from me
There's one thing not so bad,
That's knowing you'll be home again
Which always make me glad.

Separated Spouses

There are numerous reasons couples might be separated: incarceration, military service, long term illness, business reasons, immigration issues, or financial issues. Couples facing separation due to incarceration and illness may be challenged with some different dynamics than those separated for other reasons. The main issue might be centered on the issue of "consent". When considering military service, work, immigration, financial issues, or long term illness (not based on an accident) a couple usually has the opportunity to discuss the issue consenting on the separation. In giving their consent they would have agreed understanding that their sex lives will be placed on hold.

In regards to incarceration and long term illness due to accidents spouse's ability to agree to the separation may not be possible since no one anticipated the accident or the long term incarceration. After the initial arrest there is time to discuss long term incarceration before the trial. Challenges arise because of the unexpected lengthy nature of the separation. However, there are instances where a woman marries a known criminal with the understanding that he will continue committing crimes with the very real possibility he will be arrested some day.

There are so many things that could happen in regards to long term illnesses due to accidents that could hinder couple's ability to have sex such as: an accident rendering a spouse paralyzed or leaving them in a coma; a spouse being injured in combat leading to a long stay at a rehabilitative facility. No one can plan their sexual lives around the possibility that something like this will happen. Either way "consent" has a lot to do with spouse's initial agreement to remain celibate until they are reunited.

Consent is important because it gives couples time to prepare themselves emotionally to live without sex. Hopefully, the spouse who remains home can garner support from friends and family, or those in like circumstances (support groups). Even with all this support and planning there have still been instances when a couple who initially thought they could handle being separated discovered that living without sex and intimacy was more difficult than they'd surmised.

Celia Wilson

If a spouse is going to be away for an extended period of time with little to no physical contact what is a couple to do? If traveling to be together is an option, by all means make plans, save, and take full advantage of the opportunity. In some federal prisons wives are allowed to make conjugal visits. Taking advantage of them will help to keep that spark alive. Some spouses are serving life sentences and their spouses are still committed to their marriage, dedicated to their spouses.

This brings up the issue of the couple's safety: jailhouse sex and infidelity. First, don't be naïve to the fact that some incarcerated people engage in "jailhouse sex". This is sex with people of the same sex or with guards while they are incarcerated. They are not bisexual or homosexual and would never really be unfaithful, but being incarcerated and desirous of physical release (other than masturbation) they'll engage in this "jailhouse sex". Don't expect them to confess this to you. In fact, many people feel humiliated and ashamed about their behavior. It's just that their sexual needs won out over their ability to remain celibate and faithful. Understand this is usually for people locked up for long, long periods of time.

Other than the infidelity issues there are serious health consequences for the couple to consider: HIV/AIDS and Hepatitis. In order for one spouse to warn the other that they've contracted either disease, they have to know, then admit they have been unfaithful and this is usually highly unlikely. So this may be something to keep in mind when considering whether to remain married to a spouse who's going to be incarcerated for a long time. The spouse who remains at home might also want to keep in mind that contracting a venereal disease is a real possibility if they are unfaithful while their spouse is incarcerated.

Sometimes, a spouse can get use to acts of oral sex or masturbation with long term incarceration. Quite honestly it is often difficult for them to conform once again to conventional sex with their spouse once they return home. Again, they may not be able to voice this fact. In turn a cycle of frustration may ensue for the couple. They may think there's something wrong with them. Both of them may express this "unknowing" in frustration and anger. The only way to work through this is for the couple to openly trust each other while also seeking professional help to express what is and is not going on.

Military spouses can face deployments of a year or two realistically. People have been celibate for longer spans of time. It is possible. Widows and widowers have lived celibate lives for years with no problems. However, there have been instances of military personnel engaging in extramarital affairs during extended deployments. Children have even been conceived as a result of these liaisons. The military person returns home without disclosing the relationship or without knowing a child was conceived, only to find out later when the old lover or adult child seeks them out here in the U.S. It is quite devastating, but couples have survived even this. The key is knowing and being honest. Never hesitate to seek professional counsel when facing hard issues such as these.

  Being married to a trucker, musician, athlete, minister, or businessman who travels frequently could place wives in danger, also, if while away the husband succumbs to the wiles of groupies who target these particular groups of men. Just being aware that the potential exists could save lives. Women hang out at truck stops. Women are hired to attend business and church conferences. Women sit on the front row in churches with short skirts on with their legs open to entice ministers. Professional prostitutes frequent bars where men hold their luncheons and business meetings. Girls are brought onto golf courses. We all know women groupies follow musicians. Athletes and pilots often have women in each city they visit. Some of the more notable incidents have been in the news of late. Let it be understood all these women provide sexual favors to the men they service. It goes without saying that this behavior does not honor the

ANOINTED Married Christian Men

marriage or the couple's marriage bed, Amen.

The Single Girls Battle Cry

Lord, I know a blessing's on the way,
And Satan knows with You I'm going to stay.
But he keeps trying to make me flee,
Because Your Son has set me free.

The Devil will try to make me slip.
He thinks if I fall I'll lose my grip.
Too bad for him cause You're right there,
To protect me from all harm and every care.

Yes, the liar tries to deceive my mind,
With sins against my flesh of every kind.
But I know what You have for me,
And through patience You'll let me see.

Loving You and obeying Your Word,
The Destroyer thinks it is absurd.
But You've set a course for my life,
And one bright day I'll be a wife.

Until that day Lord please preserve,
My love and kisses for he who deserves,
To have this manifold tenderness
And the Holy union You will bless.

Celia Wilson

Newlywed

Many people imagine newlyweds jumping right into bed with a "GO" in all areas when actually the first time a couple becomes intimate can be a time of timidity and insecurity. Many women feel unsure of themselves. Thinking things like: Am I going to satisfy him? Will he like me in bed? What if I don't look right? I might make the wrong sound. What if I pass gas? What if he doesn't like some part of my body? He's going to see me nude for the first time. All sorts of thing go through our minds like: What words do I use to talk about sex, the words from the street, clinical terms? Will we use baby words or make up nick names for our body parts? Do I initiate sexual activity? If I do will he think I'm cheap, or a freak, or a whore, and he might change the way he thinks about me. Oh, it's so perplexing.

If the new bride is not a virgin (as many women aren't today – hopefully that will change) does she let her groom know how experienced she is? If so how far into the marriage should she reveal this? How much if any, should she hold back? It's a lot of pressure. If she is a virgin or has been celibate for a long time she will be nervous. Husbands have to be understanding.

Brides, our husbands may be nervous, as well. As a result they may be too anticipatory leading to premature ejaculation. Wives, we need not make

ANOINTED Married Christian Men

the incident into a big deal. They need us to soothe them, rub them, and encourage them without making them feel belittled. They will be raring to go demonstrating their male prowess in pleasing you in no time.

There's nothing like going to sleep on your wedding night unsatisfied after anticipating that honeymoon sex for so long - so husbands don't rush. Take all the time needed to satisfy yourself and your new bride. Explore her body. Don't just have sex with her body. Be intimate with her mind, body, and spirit. The Bible uses the phrases, "And he knew her", "He knew his wife" when referring to a couples sexual unity. Likewise your times of sexual expression can be used to get to "know her". Ask her what she likes. Ask her if she'd like this or that. Listen to her verbal responses to what you do to her. Listen to her body and pay attention to how she responds to what you do to her.

Now some people like hard sex; while others like gentle sex, some like wild sex, and others like all types of combination sex. There's a lifetime to learn what the other likes, so take your time. Get to "KNOW" how to please your partner sexually.
One goal equally important to both husband and wife is "NO FAKE ORGASMS." Some women have never had a true orgasm, even though they've had multiple children. Yes, that's right. It is the husband's job to PLLEEAASSSEEE his bride. It is the

brides' responsibility, to tell her husband if and when she is she is not being satisfied to show her husband how she likes to be touched, for instance. Our men aren't mind readers, therefore, we shouldn't expect them to know everything about us sexually and they shouldn't be angry if we reveal what pleases us.

Male virgins need to know some women are "multi-orgasmic", meaning they have orgasm, after orgasm, after orgasm. Don't be afraid. Be very, very happy. This means you've done a wonderful job. Be pleased with yourself, because she is. You can trust this.

Oh, here are some other little things newlyweds might want to remember regarding sex:

> A.   Keep the intimate details of your private sex life private. You'll talk about general stuff with your friends and maybe family, but the intimate details belong to no one else.
> B.   Cover yourselves in the presence of children or teens in your homes.
> C.   Install locks on your bedroom door because kids will come into your room.

The Place

All sex between married Christians does not

ANOINTED Married Christian Men

have to take place at home or in the bedroom. If the excitement of sex in the park or in the car appeals to you as a couple go for it. Sex in public places like elevators, or planes, and restaurants, etc. can be enticing, but they are also dangerous, because if caught the couple could face criminal charges. This would dishonor the couple.

While some of these adventurous couples will continue their sexual adventures others may prefer to engage in fondling and petting in public places, like a husband manually pleasuring his wife under a table at a wedding or something like that. It's fun for them. No one knows and it spices up their sex life. If they were ever caught it would be dishonoring to their marriage as marital sex is sacred and private.

Some couples have sex on their or their friends and families porches, decks, in their backyards on swings, or in their bathrooms. Sneaking a good time like this has been done and enjoyed immensely by couples.

Celia Wilson

Prayer for You (IV)

ANOINTED Married Christian Men

    Heavenly Father, I praise you and magnify Your Holy Name. I love You, Lord. I pray You forgive me for anything and everything I did or thought that was wrong. Father, I forgive everyone, including myself of any wrong I feel was done to me and I thank You for forgiving me, Lord.
    Heavenly Father, I pray for our sex life, Lord. If our sex drives are not in sync, I pray You put them in sync. I pray You teach us how to please each other. I pray You help me to really forgive my spouse if he has been unfaithful. Help me, Lord, to put aside my will, my pride, and my fear regarding sex with _____, if I know he is healthy. Help me to love, not in word only, but in deed and in truth. Help me, Lord, to not keep sexual secrets from my spouse, the kind that would put our lives at risk. Help me to face myself and seek professional assistance if I need to grow or be healed of anything negatively affecting my sexual performance with _____.
    Father, I want _____ to know how appealing and satisfying sex is with him. I want to be exciting and excited being with him. Use me holistically to please, pleasure, and fulfill _____ sexual needs, Lord, so _____ won't be distracted or enticed by other women.
    I take authority over every spirit of adultery, lust, sexual perversion that would hinder, harm, or destroy our marriage and the sex we have within our marriage. I thank you that my desire is

for_____ and _____ is ever satisfied at my breasts.

Forgive me, Lord, if I've been mean, hateful, resentful, or used sex as a weapon. I apologize. Please heal me from any bitterness that may have formed as a result of _____ inability to bring me to orgasm or his ability to maintain an erection. Heal him, Lord. Help him to face himself and seek professional assistance, if needed. Forgive us if we've said or done things to hurt one another regarding sex or if there's something impacting our sex life negatively.

Lord, let our sex life become a ministry to one another to honor You. Let our love for each other manifest itself demonstratively within our sexual expressions to one another, physically, emotionally, and spiritually.

I thank You, Lord, for keeping _____ from any evil people who would entice him to commit adultery breaking his vow to You and me, in Jesus' Mighty Name, Amen.

Need

I need you. You need me.
We need God.

God loves you. God loves me.
In God we both are free.

Free to live. Free to love.
Free to laugh. Free to give.

Free to become one in our mutual love.

CHAPTER 8
ANOINTED HUSBANDS AND OUR KIDS

Statistics on Child Predators

According to this website, http://www.cpiu.us, the following data exists:

- For the vast majority of child victimizers in State prison, the victim was someone they knew before the crime.
- A third had committed their crime against their own child; about half had a relationship with the victim as a friend, acquaintance, or relative other than offspring. About 1 in 7 reported the victim to have been a stranger to them.
- Three-quarters of the violent victimizations of children took place in either the victim's home or the offender's home.
- One of every seven victims of sexual assault reported to law enforcement was under age 6.
- 3 in 4 child victims of violence were female.
- 3 in 10 child victimizers reported that they had committed their crimes against multiple victims; they were more likely than those who victimized adults to have had multiple victims.
- Inmates who victimized children were less likely than other inmates to have a prior criminal record–nearly a third of child-victimizers had never been arrested prior to the current offense, compared to less than 20% of those who victimized adults.
- Sixty-seven percent of all victims of sexual

assault reported to law enforcement agencies were juveniles (under the age of 18) 34% of all victims were under age 12.

Teach the Children

Teach the children how to pray.
Teach them Jesus is The Way.
Lay your hands upon their heads,
And bless them as they go to bed.

For Jesus hears those little prayers,
And for them all He really cares.
So teach the children how to pray,
And from His path they will not stray.

ANOINTED Married Christian Men

    For many Christian women finding a Christian husband to either have children with or to help raise their children is an answer to much prayer. They've envisioned an orderly home, a strong leader, and a family covered with the prayers of a Godly loving man all within the confines of a covenant marriage. These desires are not farfetched or foolish, especially, in a time when divorce leaves many children without a father in the home. Similarly, many children lack a father's influence in the home due to death, drug use, incarceration, and the fact that many women have children out of wedlock. So anyone can understand why it's reasonable for these women to rejoice when a Christian man proposes.

    However, there are several areas these Christian women may not consider or may overlook in their zeal to obtain their dreams of Godly marriages. Why would these women overlook anything when all they desire is a blessed marriage like they hear preached from the pulpit? The reason lies in the fact that today families include her kids, his children, their children, and foster or adopted children all combined to complete this family. So the aspects of parenting children involves firm, fair, and consistent discipline, helping children discover their purpose, education, employment, or business choices, all while recognizing and preventing Pedophilia and other abuses, keeping their children alive, among other topics.

    Today many married couples already have

Celia Wilson

children by other people before they wed. This matters because the couple will have some decisions to make regarding discipline. It's important that all discipline be meted out fairly and age appropriately for all children, regardless of how they entered the family. Discipline is correction, instruction, support, encouragement, understanding, empathy, caring, etc. In the Purposeful Parenting Program created by this author parents learn there are 76 ways to discipline a child before ever putting a belt or a hand on them. However, a child/adolescent/teen's temperament and personality will bear directly on the form of discipline parents choose to administer. Whatever form of discipline is choosen parents should decide as a team. Not doing so can be devastating to the children and the family's stability.

Let's peruse some examples of abusive parents:

1. A woman is pregnant before she gets married. She doesn't tell her new husband before they get married and they raise her son as their own. When he is a toddler the husband notices the child doesn't look like him, but he nor his wife say anything about it. The husband kicks the child in the butt knocking him to the ground on numerous occasions. Everyone laughs it off. The mother doesn't step in to protect her son. The husband says supposedly funny things to the child, but they're really hurtful. Another son is born into this family

fathered by this man, resembling this man. This child's looks make the differences in the other son's appearance more apparent. As the two son's reach their teenage years the eldest child is spoken to negatively, but the younger son is always praised. The first son ends up on drugs and in jail, while the younger son is gainfully employment and in college long before he even graduates high school.

2. A woman has a daughter before she is married. After their marriage she and her husband have another daughter. From the time the two girls can walk and talk the eldest daughter is always blamed and accused of anything that goes wrong by the younger daughter's father. The mother doesn't intercede on her daughter's behalf. Instead she chimes in with her husband berating the girl. The first daughter ends up getting in fights all the time and is described as angry by her mother because she feels the teen disrespects her. The couple divorces and the daughter's relationship is let's say strained.

What can Christian women glean from these examples?

- Avoid sex before marriage or at least use protection to avoid pregnancy.
- If you get pregnant before marriage and you know tell your fiancé – even if you know it's not his or you aren't sure who's the father.
- Don't be afraid to be incensed about

anyone abusing your child. Go to your child, tell them they've done nothing wrong. Hold them, hug them, and tell them to tell you if they're ever treated in this manner again, especially when you can't see them or they are out of your sight.

- Speak up for your child when your husband becomes abusive or excessive.
- Speak to your husband about his rearing of your children.
- Avoid favoring one child over another.
- Avoid verbal comparisons between your kids.
- Develop a fair way to discipline your kids when you're not sure which child is responsible for an incident.
- Praise all your children regularly.
- If your husband abuses the kids insist he obtains professional/spiritual counseling.
- If he refuses to go to counseling do whatever is best to protect your child/ren, which may mean leaving him and/or reporting the abuse.

The worst thing we as women can do is assume our secret will never be revealed if we remain silent. *For nothing is secret that will not be revealed, nor anything hidden that will not be known and come to light.* (Luke 8:16-18)

ANOINTED Married Christian Men

3.	Here is another example where the new wife showed her children favoritism over her new husband's teenage son. A divorced father remarried taking his eldest teenage son into his new marriage to a woman with 2 pre-teens. She wouldn't allow her husband's son to get anything out of the refrigerator, while her kids could. Her refusal to allow him access to the refrigerator differs from parents trying to quell teenagers' often ravenous appetites. She made her husband's son sleep in the garage, while her husband supported her decisions. Now this is different from a teen requesting the garage be converted in a room so he can have some privacy. She showed a total disregard for his personhood from the beginning of their interactions. This woman made concerted efforts to alienate her husband's son. She made concentrated efforts to separate him from "her" family. This example shows us that husband's are not the only ones who can perpetuate mistreatment of children. Women, wives, and mothers can abuse, too. Husbands in these situations have the same options we listed earlier. By the way the young man in this example became a very successful entrepreneur, probably due to his strong secure self image, which he received from his parents before he was subjected to his step-mother.

4.	In another example a young mother has 2 toddlers, a girl and a boy. These babies act out sex acts and the little girl has a vaginal discharge. What would you say to this? These kids have seen someone having sex in person or on T.V., maybe even in print or on the Internet. This should not be. Sadly, they probably have been sexually abused by someone their mother knows. She never took them to the doctor to find out why the baby had a discharge or to receive counseling.

Key things here for mothers to remember:

- Avoid having sex when the kids are in the room.
- Don't let babies watch sex acts on T.V.
- Please, watch your kids, being mindful of who's around them because most child abusers will be someone they know or someone who knows you.
- Lastly, if little kids have any type of discharge from their sexual organs take them to the doctor.

5. How about the young mother really on fire for the Lord who goes over her friend's house to pray and seek the Lord? She sends her little 5 or 6 year old daughter to watch T.V. with her friends 4 children, one of whom was a teenage girl. This mom thought her daughter would be safe, after all she was right downstairs in a Christian home. She didn't think that her friend's daughter would go to sleep leaving her baby alone with a teenage predator. She finds out about seventeen years later that this young

man fondled her daughter that night. Although, this mother taught her daughter to tell her if anyone touched her inappropriately and she routinely asked her if she had been violated, this little girl still didn't tell her mother. It became a repressed memory which surfaced after her daughter gave birth to her first child. It was a tumultuous recollection.
What can we learn from this poignant tale?

- Don't ever let your eagerness to get close to God lead you to neglect, to avoid watching the precious children God has blessed you with.
- If you can't pray while your little ones are in the room with you when you're visiting friends you don't need to pray, right then.
- Kids won't always tell you they've been abused, even when you teach them they should.
- There may not always be signs of the abuse, so be vigilant to watch them as much as possible.
- Don't assume that because you're involved in a spiritual endeavor with Christian people your kids are safe.

Be aware that this young man who was raised in the church was never convicted, has no record, and is still out there free to prey on other females. He is not the only one.

6. Here's another example:

Celia Wilson

A couple of women who already had children married Christian men. Their husbands worked in church, but at the same time they were putting holes in their step-daughters closets, placing mirrors under the bathroom doors to try to peek at their step-daughters in various states of undress. They'd go outside when the girls dressed or undressed to peek at them through the blinds or through the sides of the curtains to try and see them naked. They are voyeurs.

Lessons to be learned by these women's stories:

- If your husband leaves the room every time your daughter or son bathes, uses the bathroom, dresses, or undresses you need to find out where he is going.
- Check your kids closet doors for holes. Make sure when they dress or undress closet doors are shut. Today with the invention of spy cams check your kid's rooms for them or install some yourself to spy on him.
- Make sure their curtains are not transparent and cover the entire window. Remember, you can see through the mini blinds.
- Make sure everyone receives counseling and follow the therapists' decisions after they've assessed your husband.

This sort of abuse can have lastly physiological

effects on your children.

7. What about some foster dads abusing their foster daughters, even after raising their own daughters without any problems?

Lesson to learn here:

- Don't assume that since he raised your kids he won't abuse someone else's child.

8. What about the wonderful family (father, mother, and kids). There is only one girl in the family. As an adult she says she was consistently sexually assaulted by a family member. We later learn that family member was her eldest brother. She had female problems all her life and became an alcohol and drug abuser to hide the pain and shame. She received treatment, but she is forever troubled that her now grown brother will abuse other girls. Remember this man has never been arrested for this repeated abuse. There are others like him walking around.

What can be taken away from this alarming account?

- Be mindful of where you choose to put your daughter's bedroom in relation to all others.
- Check on your children throughout the night.
- Don't assume siblings won't molest each other.

9. Another account rests with the military father

who abused his own son. He'd fly him to places and rape him until one day he told his mother.

What can be taken away from this?

- Don't assume your husband won't rape his own son.
- Don't let the uniform he wears convince you he won't molest.

10. Here's an account about a teenage girl who told a group facilitator at her high school her mom's live-in-boyfriend was repeatedly raping her, but she would never tell her mother because they'd have to move out of their nice home and give up purchasing all the name brand clothes they wore. Plus, if she told she wouldn't be able to get her nails and hair done all due to the two incomes her mom and the boyfriend brought into the home. Does anyone wonder why this young lady was angry, fought all the time, and had failing grades?

What does this story reveal?

- Just because your kids aren't telling you, doesn't mean abuse is not taking place.
- Refrain from letting your boyfriend live with you and your children.

11. Maybe your boyfriend doesn't profess to be a man of faith. What if you already know he's a bad guy? What if you know his crime is that he's a convicted sex offender? There are women who bring men into their homes knowing their boyfriends have a history of sexual abuse, rape, etc. This should be

avoided, period. After he has abused your kids you'll be charged with child endangerment because you knowingly put your children in danger.

This little snippet brings a warning.

- Investigate these men before you start dating them.
- Don't bring every guy you meet around your kids.

12. What about the young adolescent male repeatedly sexually abused by various female friends of the family and female relatives? Many young guys, and older ones too for that matter, think that a young guy having sex or being broken in by an older women is something to brag about. They think it is a sign of manhood or a sign he's desirable. However, the truth is distinctly different because these women are committing a crime and what they are doing is ABUSIVE and damaging to the young male. He became promiscuous, fathering numerous children. He had a problem forming and committing to meaningful relationships with women. Their abuse of this young man led to his becoming a sexual addict.

Can we glean anything from this scenario?

- Don't assume that because you have a son he's safe with your female friends, family and neighbors.
- Women do abuse. It's often easier for them because what most people would

consider nurturing acts, such as sitting a child on her lap or holding a child up in her arms (like when a little girls dress covers the forearm), can all be instances when a woman actually fondles a child. What about a female relative or babysitter lying on a bed with a child to get her/him to go to sleep? Is this an opportunity for abuse? There was an instance when adolescent girls were fondled by their adolescent female cousin as they napped. Their cousin was a victim of sexual abuse herself. So don't just think sexual abuse is committed by men.

13.   Our last story of abuse is about a step-father who would wake his teenage step-daughter up in the morning when she was reluctant to get up for school by kicking her in the behind while cursing her out. Of course she woke up angry and in pain so she reacted by hitting him back. At this aggression he in turn punched her in the face like he was punching a man. Then people wondered why she had problems fighting in school.

These real stories about real people impacted real children's lives. God is holding us accountable for the health and wellbeing of our children. Wanting a spouse, needing a man, or the fact that our loins are on fire can't take precedence over them. Did you know that the majority of youth in juvenile correctional facilities have mental health issues? Our behavior or lack thereof directly impacts our kid's mental health. We don't want them to end up adjudicated, do we? We don't want them to commit suicide, do we? Then we have to wake up to these realities and become proactive to protect them.

There are some characteristics those who may have plans to abuse children may exhibit:
- They may be loaners. To women this man might seem shy, which can make him appealing.
- They may spend more time with children than with their mate or potential mate.
- They are not adept at interacting with their peers.
- They many spend a lot of secretive or private time on the computer.
- They often can be found in places where children frequent and places parents trust like churches, synagogues, youth and neighborhood centers, parks and playgrounds, youth organizations, schools, and juvenile correctional facilities.
- They want to be alone with their mate's children or take them places without their mates. For women who have been single parents and feel as if they need a break this gesture may seem heaven sent

Celia Wilson

and the man like a Godsend, but beware.

As potential spouses we need to perform background checks on anyone we intend to marry, or anyone who wants to spend time with our children. Remember, many child abusers, molesters, and rapists don't have criminal records so we must be vigilant. Remembering more child abusers, molesters, and rapists will be people either we or our children are familiar with will help us protect them. So go ahead and teach them about "Stranger Danger (the danger that a stranger might be a threat to them and they should be careful)", but by all means teach them about FFD "Family and Friend Danger" (the danger family and friends can potentially pose). Teach them about appropriate and inappropriate touch. Teach them about what and where on their bodies should not be touched, even about appropriate and inappropriate pictures. No one should take pictures of your kids in different stages of undress. Tell your kids to tell you if anyone tells them, "This is just our secret." Teach them to talk to you about everyone who spends time with them.

Look and listen for signs your child has changed or that something has happened. Some signs might be: They withdraw or are depressed (sleep a lot, won't eat, won't talk to friends), they try to commit suicide, grades drop, they become aggressive or fight a lot, they become promiscuous, overly sexualized, they become angry, they start

ANOINTED Married Christian Men

drinking, using other drugs, they choose new friends, or they change their looks drastically, etc.

If your child cries when going to a particular person's home is mentioned or they say they don't want to go pay attention and ask why. If they say they don't want to go with someone start asking questions. If they say they don't like it when someone comes to your house pay attention and ask questions. Be suspicious of anyone who visits your home who always wants to go to your child's room. If someone wants to visit your children in their room go with them. Watch people who want to tickle or put their hands on your children. Also, be watchful of people who bring your children gifts. Have them give them the gifts in your presence, because sometimes these people use the gifts as a means to garner affection from your kids. Ask them regularly if they are alright. Let them know you are there, ready to talk, and listen. If they tell you someone touched them or hurt them, believe them. Don't judge or blame them. Remain calm and get all the details. Go to the authorities. Get them medical attention (physical and psychological).

If you find it difficult to start conversing about the topic maybe renting movies that cover or contain some aspect of the subject from the library is one source. Your physician or professionals in the fields of education, social work, ministry, and counseling can direct you to other useful tools to help you and

Celia Wilson

your family discuss this topic.

We can be thankful God Anointed Christian Husbands. We can be thankful our hearts desire is to be in God's perfect will. Marrying an anointed man of God who will cover us, lead our homes, and raise our children is a truly noble attainable goal. With the guidance of the Holy Spirit and our use of Godly wisdom we can fulfill our dreams, while also ensuring the safety of our children. Amen and God bless our families.

Praise God for all the men and women, fathers and mothers, step-parents, foster parents, adoptive parents, grandparents, aunts, uncles, cousins, siblings, and family friends who are loving children. Thank you for mentoring and training them; teaching and nurturing them. You are so important. You are needed and appreciated by more people than you could ever count. Thank you for keeping your kids safe and endeavoring to make them happy, well adjusted young people. Thank you, God Bless you. Amen.

ANOINTED Married Christian Men

Celia Wilson

blurb.com